Arthur G. James, M.D.
Surgeon With A Dream

By George W. Paulson, M.D. and Kristin Rodgers, M.L.I.S.

©Copyright 2009, All Rights Reserved.
Published by James Property Management, Ltd. LLC
Cover painting by Kathy Calderone Sochor ©1998, used with permission.

ISBN: 978-0-692-00112-7

TABLE OF CONTENTS

Preface v

Chapter	Page

1) Parents and Early Life 1
2) Medical School 18
3) Internship and Marriage 25
4) Military 34
5) Cancer Training 42
6) Return to Columbus 52
7) OSU and James 75
8) Columbus Cancer Clinic 79
9) American Cancer Society 97
10) Travel as a Mission 106
11) Academician 111
12) Surgeon 123
13) Friends 130
14) Investor 141
15) Accolades 148
16) The Dream Becomes Concrete 155
17) James Cancer Hospital Today 184
18) Last Days 197

    Conclusions 205

    References 207

    James Collection Summary 210

    Acknowledgments 222

    Index 223

    About the Authors 233

Preface

This book is the celebration of a man with a dream, and the story of what happened to the dream and to the man who had the dream. We hope the telling reveals the basis for both the dream and for the spirit of the Dreamer. Any life offers potential lessons, and certainly the life and times of this surgeon, this independent thinker, demonstrates what a single determined man can do. Others may learn from his example, and we hope this book, and his story, will uncover the bedrock for his ultimate success.

In recounting an individual's life we measure promise versus achievement, positive against negative, success contrasted to failure. We try to do this in this book, and we hope our reconstruction of Dr. Arthur James' story has wider meaning than simply offering a record for those who cherished the man, or a tribute to the institution he, more than any one person, founded. Hundreds of letters, as well as discussions with dozens of people who knew him, plus the Arthur G. James, M.D. Collection at the Medical Heritage Center (MHC) have been our resources. Many colleagues did not agree, certainly did not agree all the time, with his goals; but no one questioned his commitment, his devotion to patients, or his dignified persistence in the face of all difficulties. He was respected by all, relied upon as physician by many, and loved by those who worked most closely with him. In the writing we did try to avoid whitewash or hagiography. We admit we admire the man we describe, but nothing has been deliberately suppressed by us or by others. We failed to find anything of significance to criticize about this man. We can accept that good men did, and do, exist. And perhaps that is our real story.

A single man **can** matter, of course. Our subject, Arthur G. James, M.D., was the product of a hard working and devoted Italian immigrant family who came to a country that allows potential to flourish. Early in life he developed a life focusing dream. Perhaps as a young medical student he once dreamed of curing cancer. In the end he simply resolved to build the best cancer hospital in America. He came close. Even if this book is about him, as the visionary, it is also about his dream hospital. Inevitably, since the book involves medicine and academia, it is about attentive patient care, about mentoring and the transmission of excellence, qualities that are hallmarks of good medical teaching.

It is clear that numerous individual physicians have left lasting marks. The Mayo Brothers (Mayo, C.W.) accelerated the idea of group practice, and proved inspired leadership can build a model program in unlikely places – Rochester, Minnesota. Other physicians, Drs. Alton Ochsner (Wilds, J. and Harkey, I.) in New Orleans and George Crile (Crile) in Cleveland, also demonstrated that busy surgeons could establish a clinic that grew to include non surgeons, and the resultant institutions now raise funds for research and philanthropic care. The founders interacted so successfully with other medical disciplines that their programs outstripped and outlasted anything surgical the surgeons ever dreamed of. Other surgeons, men such as Dr. Ernest Amory Codman (Mallow, W.J.) in Boston, despite odds and the disdain of colleagues, forever elevated ethical record keeping. Sir William Osler (Bliss, M.) remains a demigod of clinical medicine, and admirers meet yearly to discuss the example of mentoring he offered to generations of physicians. Yes, individuals such as James matter greatly in medical education, and for optimal medical care. Medicine remains "a hands-on" discipline and much of its teaching is still by apprenticeship and with a mentor.

Medicine in America is regional, and Ohio has its own unique tradition of competent and compassionate medical care. Such quality care is as characteristic of Columbus, Ohio, as it is in any section of America. Quality began early in our history, as is documented in <u>The</u>

<u>Second Blessing: Columbus Medicine and Health The Early Years</u> written by Dr. Charles Wooley and Barbara Van Brimmer. Their title was taken from a quotation by Izaak Walton, with the first blessing being a good conscience, the second good health. Columbus has had good health, and the blessing of having many good doctors. We have memorialized several local medical leaders, thanks to the Medical Heritage Center established by joint action of The Ohio State University (OSU) and the Columbus Medical Association. Examples of such publications from the MHC include monographs about Dr. J. H. J. Upham (1871-1960), the dean who preserved the medical school (Wooley and Van Brimmer), and James F. Baldwin, (1850-1936) the energetic curmudgeon and professor who built Grant Hospital (Paulson). Arthur G. James, M.D., (1912-2001) is another such worthy to remember.

    There are aspects of this book that receive less emphasis than the story of the man and his sustained effort to build what became the "Arthur G. James Cancer Hospital and Richard J. Solove Research Institute." The hospital itself is unique in several ways, including its role as the leader in cancer research for the state. It is an example of one of the first hospitals in town organized around a disorder, not reflecting all disorders as in a general hospital, a particular discipline, or for any one special group such as children or women. Another notable aspect of the hospital, and of James himself, is the innovative efforts at translational, multidisciplinary, therapy and research which began well before such cooperative programs became a national thrust. But the book is really about the man and about his dream, not primarily about the hospital, remarkable as it may be. The readers can decide for themselves whether the man we describe was just too good to be true. We do believe most will agree, at any rate, that he was extraordinary.

This book presents James' story in a largely chronological pattern, organized in subsections of interest. The authors readily admit being subject to the favorable bias implied earlier, and James successfully operated on the son of one author (GP). We recognize that any biographer might be expected to turn up dark corners, misdeeds, or peccadilloes that reveal feet of clay in the subject. In that we failed. We have identified no public scandals, no rages in the operating room, and no medical misadventures, only sustained loyalty to and from family, friends, and patients. There was not even a malpractice suit to titillate the reader. Above all there was the overarching canopy of his fight against cancer and the push toward a cancer hospital. Almost everyone we interviewed felt he was reliable, kind, conscientious, self-confident, competent, and a public and private servant of exemplary virtue and deliberate humility.

The primary source for the book is the carefully organized Arthur G. James, M.D. Collection retained in the MHC, and summarized after the concluding chapters. Kristin Rodgers, M.L.I.S., served as the Project Archivist from September 2006 to October 2007 and processed the collection. Clara Jacobs, R.N., youngest sister of James, and his two sons, David and Cameron, were generous with information and supplied many of the illustrations used. Norma Flesher, R.N., James' nurse/secretary for four decades, not only saved and helped organize the collection, but offered many, even sweet, personal memories of her boss. More than one person said: "You really ought to write the book about Norma, she is a saint." Almost a hundred people commented or recalled aspects of James' long and prolific life. Several, including Professors John Burnham, Ph.D., and Manuel Tzagournis, M.D., reviewed most of the manuscript. Professor Thomas Minnick supplied editorial assistance. Dennis Mathias designed the book and offered wise counsel. Some of those who helped are listed at the end, but there is no way to thank all adequately.

Much of this book reflects their collective memory, and we hope that will serve as the best thanks.

References to the Arthur G. James, M.D. Collection in the MHC are by box number, or box number and specific folder within the box, such as (JC 54) or (114/18). Other references are presented in more standard fashion.

We dedicate this book to all whose lives have been blessed by the Arthur G. James Cancer Hospital and Richard J. Solove Research Institute.

George W. Paulson, M.D.   Kristin R. Rodgers, M.L.I.S.

"When I was a child my parents spoke only Italian at home."

Arthur G. James, M.D.

Chapter 1
Parents and Early Life: the Dreamer learns of his roots

Name and Birth

We knew him as "Arthur G. James," but his family and the professors in medical school initially knew him as Arthur David Giangiacomo. His medical school classmate, Donald J. Vincent, M.D., remembered their professors were fond of calling out for "Mr. Giangiacomo," and some let the vowels trail off their tongues. The Ohio State University Archives records that in December 1934, during his first year as a member of the medical class of 1937, the future Dr. James legally changed his last name from Giangiacomo, meaning son of James, to James. His mother agreed the name change was appropriate, and at the insistence of his father all the family eventually changed their name. Even the given names for some of the children evolved from that of an earlier Italian ancestor into an "Americanized" form. James chose to retain "Giangiacomo," as his middle name.

Young Arthur was born on March 14, 1912, in Rhodesdale, a town in Southeastern Ohio that no longer exists down in the foothills of Appalachia. James said his birthplace was in Belmont County (109/12). There is still a Rhodesdale in Maryland, and perhaps the early Ohio settlers who established Rhodesdale, Ohio, remembered roots in the east. Rhodesdale and the town the family briefly moved to next, Tappan, both vanished when the local coal mines petered out.

James' Parents

Achieving a true maturity implies acceptance of responsibility for our actions and our ambitions, combined with adult acceptance of our roots and our inheritance. James was always proud of his roots, and his DNA must have been exceptional. He was the third of nine children of Italian immigrants, Abramo Giangiacomo (1877-1964) and Rosa Pezzopane (1884-1960) (137/13). Abramo and Rosa came from the country town of Onna, near L'Aquila, the provincial capital of the Italian Province of Abbruzzo. Onna is 80 miles, about two hours, from Rome. The "Abramo story," as recounted by the surviving ninth child, Mrs. Clara Jacobs, was a remarkable tale of restless independence, courage, and adaptability. Abramo ran away from home at age 13, was retrieved, but ran away again at age 14. He feared it was destined for him to become a soldier, since all Italian youths were expected to serve. For a short time Abramo became a laborer in Germany, and then he was in Somalia. In the European scramble for colonies in Africa at the end of the nineteenth century, Italy, which had only recently become united, claimed influence in southern Somalia.

When the adventuresome Abramo came to America he preferred not to live in New York because, or so Mrs. Jacobs said, there was potential influence of the "Black Hand Gang." In fact the Black Hand Gang was an assassination group in Europe and probably not a big problem at Ellis Island, but there were certainly people who preyed on recent immigrants. Surely by the time Abramo arrived in America caution as well as exploration were forever included in his survival skills. After a stint in upstate New York working on the Niagara Falls

Abramo Giangiacomo (Courtesy of James Family)

power generating project, he went west and south to seek a job in Ohio. He returned from the coal mines of Ohio to Onna three years later as a mature young man, and after he saw the beautiful black haired Rosa walking with her father, he asked the parents to arrange a wedding. They did so, and the couple was married in the church on the square.

What was their original home town of Onna like? James, who visited Italy several times, described it as a neat village of perhaps 100 families, with an impressive square and rugged scenery. It is still a small village of modest stone and masonry homes, with sheep nearby and family gardens. The church where Rosa and Abramo were married in 1907 still stands in the square and still serves for weddings. Skiing is now possible nearby, and tourist visits are common. When family members from America went from little Onna to visit nearby L'Aquila they saw medieval walls and a major college town of perhaps 40,000 people tucked deep into the rugged hills of the spine of Italy.

Church in Onna (Courtesy of James Family)

James' Parents Come to America

The couple arrived in America in 1907, along with the flood of Italian immigrants of the time. On the way to America they stopped at Milano, Mrs. Jacobs related, attended two operas at the La Scala Opera House, and even visited Paris as well. Abramo resumed work in the coal mines that were opening up all over Ohio; mines were particularly rich in the foothills of Appalachia. Rosa had displayed her love and courage by accompanying Abramo to the distant land, but after several children were born she was not adjusting well and had recurrent abdominal distress which she attributed to the strange water. So the little family packed up and returned to Onna. It is not clear how comfortable it was living back in Onna, they were under the eyes of extended families, and the time was unsettled internationally. Soon it looked inevitable that war (World War I) would engulf all Europe, and Abramo was at risk to be swept up into the Italian army. His passport was at hand, so he returned to America and the coalfields of Ohio. Rosa stayed behind in Onna.

What followed suggests that Rosa was as remarkable as her husband. For three months or so she continued to live in Onna with their three children, including Arthur, in a house James could still visit in 1973 (JC 54 and Jacobs). Rosa stayed under the protection of her parents until arrangements to return to America were finalized. Her trip from Italy and to Ellis Island, then on by train, was a nightmare, and she told Clara Jacobs, her last child, that it was the most difficult time of her life. She was pregnant again, and when she got to the shores of America the children with her were placed in quarantine for three weeks because they had measles. But eventually they did return to Ohio, and she resumed her busy life near St. Clairsville in Belmont County.

Life in America

Rosa, or Rose, is remembered as a kind and skillful mother and as a magnificent cook. Home made pastas and almost innumerable sauces for spaghetti were the rule. When asked years later what was his favorite food, James answered readily, "homemade spaghetti," and Mrs. Mildred James made sure her mother-in-law taught her the true mysteries of Italian cuisine.

Abramo and Rosa had only four years of education, but she was bright and organized, and he was good with figures, careful with money, and superb at planning. Even in his old age he made the stock market work for him, despite occasional financial losses. According to James, Abramo used his hard earned wages to invest in a grocery store and then bought another one near the Crabapple Mine, 15 miles away (109/12). Work in the stores kept all eight children busy. The Giangiacomo grocery stores were near their home, located then in Uniontown, and home was close to the two-room school. There is another Uniontown in northeastern Ohio, but both the grocery stores

Art and local saleman at the James' family grocery store (Courtesy of James Family)

and the family home in Uniontown were located in the village close to St. Clairsville, the county seat of Belmont County, and just off Route I-70 before one crosses the river to Wheeling, West Virginia. St. Clairsville is named for Arthur St. Clair, physician, general, and briefly governor of the Ohio territory and; the use of the Arthur name for James is probably a coincidence.

Arthur remembered his father going over the books on the kitchen table at night, with Rosa by his side. Young Arthur actually worked part time in another store, one basically run for the miners. That store eventually was also bought by Abramo. In that area of Ohio sons of miners were expected to join their fathers in the mines. Not so the children of the Giangiacomo couple. They were programmed to work and expected to study. Arthur later recounted a painful switching administered when he failed to return to the store to work because he had dallied to watch a baseball game.

The pool hall attached to the store burned, the home was damaged and reconstruction was needed. The family was housed temporarily by neighbors, in that time when neighbors readily offered rural good will. David, oldest son of James, remembered visiting Uniontown and meeting one of the elderly women who took in his grandparents and their children. When his father saw how much the good neighbor loved listening to the radio, tuned to the presidential convention of the time, he later purchased a TV as a token repayment for her kindness.

Abramo's skill at merchandizing was transferred to Columbus in 1936 when most of the residual family came to live on Neil Avenue. He eventually bought a grocery store at Livingston and Lockbourne Road. Felix, who had completed an engineering degree at The Ohio State University (OSU) but who remained unemployed as the Great Depression got underway, helped run that store, just as he and Arthur had done as children. But it was no longer necessary, as it once was, for

As was typical in America for hard working and devoted immigrant parents, Abramo and Rosa were absolutely determined that all of their children would be better educated than they had been. Arthur and his father met with the high school principal, and when offered the choice of a "commercial course" or a "college preparatory course," his father proudly announced: "He's a gonna go to college," James later recalled (138/22).

Father and mother were successful in their push for all the children, and there were eight to feed and educate. In sequence these were Grace, Felix, Arthur, Elizabeth, Leona, Lillian, Vincent and Clara. Before Vincent was born there was an earlier Clara, but she had died in the fire at age 3 (124/30, Jacobs and David James). As was traditional, the next child born of the same sex as the deceased received the honored name. The names do not sound particularly Italian, but several were adapted from the Italian name of earlier members of the family. In fact the names do not sound particularly Catholic, either.

James Family, c. 1923-1924, Art second from right (Medical Heritage Center, Arthur G. James, MD Collection)

The family actually attended the Presbyterian Church in Uniontown. Rosa was allowed to baptize the oldest child into the Catholic Church, but due to some unpleasant earlier experiences in his youth, Abramo refused to support the Catholic Church when they were in America.

Tradition was important to this family, but so was assimilation. All of the older children could speak some Italian, and James was able to translate in the 1970s when he visited cancer centers in Italy. The younger children understood Italian adequately, but, as is common, they answered their parents in English. They were in America after all, education was the iron key to the golden door, and all the children were expected to both fit in and to achieve advanced education. Family ties remain strong to this day, and Mrs. Jacobs recalled recent reunions that included most of the twenty-three grandchildren with a total of 106 relatives, including two adopted members of the clan. The reunions continued after the death of the original immigrants, and the earlier reunions were surely pleasant for the elderly couple, who in later

Rosa and Abramo James' 50th wedding anniversary, Art second from right (Courtesy of James Family)

years lived in Upper Arlington, a suburb of Columbus, where Abramo tended a lush garden. Rosa, born on March 13, 1884, died of bronchopneumonia on January 11, 1960. Abramo, born December 22, 1877, had late life Parkinson's disease but according to the death certificate died of stomach cancer on July 31, 1964. They are buried in Union Cemetery and rest now in the grave closest to their son's former office on Olentangy River Road.

Parent's grave in Union Cemetery (Coutesy of George Paulson, MD)

Arthur's School Success

Arthur was co-valedictorian, along with Adrian Robson, for the senior class at St. Clairsville High School. The 95-year-old Mrs. Jessie Pollock recalled her memory of "Art's" friendship with a boy who later was Congressman Wayne Hays, (1911-1989) and who rode on the bus with Art to school. She stated that Art graduated with top honors, and she wrote: "He also was Business Manager of our High School Annual book for 1929-1930. Extremely kind, he always was ready to help others with their problems. He was admired because of his soft–

spoken, gentlemanly manners. This, coupled with a great sense of humor, made him very popular, always surrounded by 'fans.' Being handsome, humble, and very bright didn't lessen his popularity either."

Art at age 17 (Medical Heritage Center, Arthur G. James, MD Collection)

She added: "Art was a spirited Italian boy who, on rare occasions just <u>had</u> to play tricks on his laboratory buddies. One I still remember vividly. Art was conducting an experiment, something with batteries, poles, etc., and he asked, 'Jessie, will you help me here?' Of course I stumbled over myself in my haste to be of help to Art! He showed me where to hold my finger between the rods – then he threw the switch! It was a mild jolt, but my screams bounced off the walls! Every one, including the teacher, who was our High School Principal, got a big laugh! Art apologized, saying he knew that Jessie would not mind. That lab class was the most fun I had in book learning, and I almost failed it, goofing around!"

In the yearbook for the graduating class of 1930 the facetious list of predictions, from "garter salesman" to "future mayor," suggested Arthur Giangiacomo would become the "Dictator of Italy." In fact Mussolini already had that job. 1930 was just before Neville Chamberlain became Chancellor of the Exchequer of England, a hint of what was to come in Europe, as was the development of a new processed form of meat, called Spam, which soldiers just over a decade later learned to eat to live and loved to hate. 1930 was a year the Yankees won the World Series, once again. More promising for the future of cancer research, in 1930 it was discovered that magnetic resonance imaging could lead to measurements of atoms and molecules. Young Arthur could not have known it then, but that advance would help his patients five decades later.

James did not participate in many extracurricular activities. He probably had no time. Nevertheless, and typical for him, he maintained many of the friendships from high school, counseled high school friends when they were ill, and was chosen to address the class at the 50-year reunion. One classmate, John Shannon, not only praised James in the local newspaper, but wrote to him later about the class, and once sought help for his wife's Alzheimer's disease. James corresponded with, gave supportive speeches, and sent money for political campaigns of Hays, the boy he once sat next to on the school bus. Democratic Congressman Hays, once a commissioner in Belmont County, was popular and extremely powerful in the halls of the Capitol, until touched by scandal involving a secretary who stated she could neither type nor file. Both men retained a lifetime interest in Belmont County. James' correspondence files include efforts to limit strip mining for coal in Belmont County (112/27), mixed with the many letters comforting members of his school class following the death of their relatives. Several times, and usually on behalf of others, for example when a urological resident at OSU was hoping to retrieve his wife from Libya, James asked Hays for help, and got it. Loyalty ran deep in those who grew up in the foothills of Appalachia.

In the 1930s, OSU awarded a first-year scholarship to any class valedictorian. Arthur Giangiacomo enrolled in The Ohio State University in Columbus in 1930, holder of such a tuition scholarship, and ready to begin his advanced education.

James' Interest in Surgery

It is impossible to know exactly when Arthur became firmly convinced the effort to cure cancer was his life's work, but the time of his commitment to become a surgeon is certain. He said his interest in surgery as a career began at age fourteen, when he was in the eighth grade, after Dr. William S. Fulton (1873-1938) successfully operated on his beloved mother Rosa and relieved her of the pains from gallstones (137/8). It must not have been the strange water of Belmont County that sent her back to Italy after all. She had her gallbladder drained earlier, as was once commonly done, but full relief was needed, and Fulton was the man. He was born in St. Clairsville, but made his name in Wheeling, where he is listed in the local hall of fame as founder of the Wheeling Clinic. In his day, as was usual at the time, Fulton saw patients in many small towns in eastern Ohio and western Pennsylvania. He held office hours seven days a week. He is still remembered in Wheeling as a superb teacher of young surgeons.

The editorial at the time of Fulton's death, a year after James graduated from medical school, reported: "It is given to few men to lead the life of abounding usefulness and action that Dr. Fulton lived. He was indeed a rare character, and we will not look on his like again." Rosa did well after the surgery. James often mentioned the surgeon about whom he said: "Dr. Fulton's confidence, competence, and kindness made a tremendous impression on me" (149/3). So James became convinced, even before leaving home, that he was to be a surgeon.

His mother expected certain success for her son. A letter from one of the children reports Rosa said as her children left home; "they will all do well, but someday they will name a hospital for Arthur" (124/29). Perhaps she was remembering Arthur's concern when she had the surgery, while he remembered Fulton, the first of his many medical mentors.

College Life

While in college Art James, his brother Felix, and another student from St. Clairsville, Bill Lee, who married Elizabeth and became James' brother-in-law, lived for a time in an attic room on East 9th Avenue. Years later in a two-page response to a request from an eighth grade student at Wellington School in Columbus who was trying to write a paper on the topic "Why Libraries?" James answered: "During my college days I shared a second floor room with two other students. This was located at a house on 14th avenue, and you can imagine it was impossible to have any private time for study. The library is ideal for study…In caring for patients I still used the libraries a great deal."

James had his scholarship for tuition, thanks to OSU, but to pay for meals he cleared tables in Hatcher's Cafeteria on High Street. His parents were surely also helpful, and he worked in their store during summers, but we can be sure the drive to work they instilled was more indispensable than any limited financial support they could ever offer to their college student. On Saturdays in the fall he ushered for football games, glad to get the $1.00 per hour, but perhaps equally glad to see the games. He was a devoted Buckeye fan all his life.

James began at first to major in engineering, as had his older brother Felix whom he admired a great deal. But after James made a "C" in calculus he responded to his own dream, and shifted to premed. He made sure he saw no more "C's" thereafter. He graduated on June 11, 1934, with a 3.75 grade point average, good enough to be admitted to OSU Medical School.

"By the time I entered medical school, I knew I wanted to be a surgeon."

Arthur G. James, M.D.

Chapter 2
Medical School: the Dreamer begins his life's work

Medical Training Begins and the Die is Cast

James entered medical school at OSU in 1934 as one of 102 in the entering class. In contrast, in 2007, 210 students were in the entering class. There were only six women in James' class, but 92 women registered with the 210 hopefuls who entered in 2007. His medical school experience mirrored what many new students still experience. More than four decades after graduation, while offering a funeral eulogy for classmate David Dillahunt, M.D., James talked of their struggle together to dissect a smelly cadaver three afternoons a week during almost the entire freshman year.

James "pledged" with the premedical fraternity, Theta Kappa Psi, and, as was typical for him, continued later to maintain contact with fellow members. In fact the former fraternity brothers who lived in the Columbus area met regularly the first Wednesday of each month for decades after graduation. Arthur James was chosen as the medical student representative to the OSU professional inter-fraternity council. Theta Kappa Psi fraternity expired after World War II, and was briefly resurrected at the OSU College of Medicine, but that particular medical fraternity no longer exists. In medical school James never lived in fraternity housing. Most such groups served primarily for social contacts, offered cheap rent for the few who did live in the fraternity, and facilitated community use of the medical books. Most current medical students are not active in any such group.

Theta Kappa Psi Medical Fraternity, James first row, right (Medical Heritage Center, Arthur G. James, MD Collection)

It was conventional that only when they reached the third year did medical students get to glimpse patients in large numbers. One of James' pleasures was to go to the old Starling-Loving operating theatres and just sit and watch (149/3). "Even before I entered medical school I knew that I wanted to specialize in surgery. I was lucky that way, because many medical students spend years studying a particular specialty before finding out they don't really like it. So, the opportunity to observe surgery was great stuff for me. There were four large amphitheaters where doctors performed surgery, and the largest one was glassed in, so you could watch surgery without having to be scrubbed." In one interview, James revealed he and other students sneaked in a backyard cat for anesthesia and surgery. They patched the cat back up without being caught. The cat did well.

James' Exposure to Surgery and Research at OSU

Between 1932 and 1947 strong parallel but separate departments of surgery evolved at OSU. One department had an orientation toward clinical surgical care and teaching. The other was designed to be more research oriented. Clinical surgery was headed by Verne Dodd, M.D. (1881-1957). Dodd had a major influence on the young medical student, and later resident, Arthur James. James' fellow classmate, D. J. Vincent, M.D., remembered Dodd as a charismatic professor and as a gracious role model for any young doctor. Charles Meckstroth, M.D.,

James and Dr. Verne Dodd, popular surgical mentor at OSU (Medical Heritage Center, Arthur G. James, MD Collection)

later a prominent cardiovascular surgeon, stated he decided to become a physician after Dodd visited his high school classroom.

There is one proof of the lasting impact of Dodd on Mildred and Arthur James: to honor the popular mentor their second son received Dodd as his middle name. Dodd's exalted position as chief, and his pleasant professional style, made him a favorite of many in the medical school. Trustees on February 22, 1957, resolved that Dodd was: "A great personality and a true friend. High personal regard is felt for him, not only for his work and as a surgeon and for teaching, but because of his personal traits, ability, and uninhibited cheerful willingness to guide young physicians in the formative years of their professions."

At the time James was in medical school there was an alternative and somewhat autonomous surgical department entitled the Department of Medical and Surgical Research headed by George Morris Curtis, M.D., Ph.D. Curtis was made full professor in 1932, and became founder of the new department in 1936. That department was terminated soon after Curtis had a stroke and could no longer continue as chairman. Curtis was productive in research, and published more than 200 research papers as well as several major monographs. His particular interest was in iodine metabolism and diseases of the thyroid. The research career of Curtis began fairly soon after iodine supplements had been proven, in the 1920s, to be the best preventive of much of the thyroid disease that existed along the "goiter belt" of the Great Lakes region.

As a student James worked during part of the summers in the lab with Curtis, and thereby earned a Master of Medical Sciences degree in addition to the M.D. degree, both awarded on June 14, 1937. In fact he managed to graduate from medical school in three years. His thesis at graduation reported studies on patients who lost iodine in the urine following surgery of several types. There had been a concept that

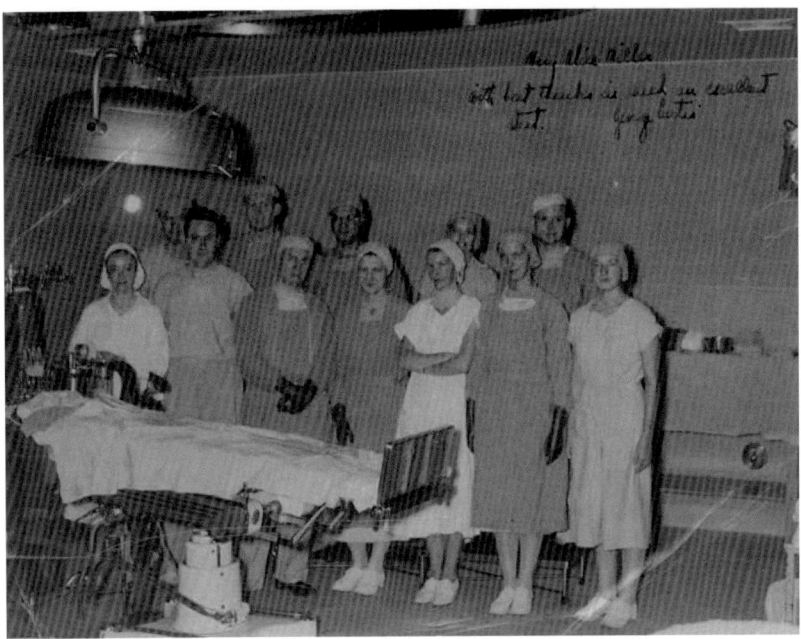

First operation (thyroidectomy) at the new University Hospital performed by Dr. George Curtis, gloves in front, along with Drs. Jay Jacoby to Curtis' right and Charles Meckstroth over his right sholder on June 28, 1951 (Medical Heritage Center, Arthur G. James, MD Collection)

iodine in substantial amounts was lost during, or just after, thyroid surgery. Young student James proved that any major surgery, not just thyroid surgery, could produce a similar loss.

Years later Dr. and Mrs. James often visited the Curtis home in Bexley, and probably they could not help admiring the widow Lucille Curtis, who had been the first woman field officer in the Foreign Service, and who served in Switzerland, Panama, and Haiti. The vivacious daughter of Lucille and George Curtis, Charlotte, wrote books and was a prominent journalist. A biography described her as the highest paid woman who ever worked for the New York Times (Greenwald). Charlotte eventually married the chief of the neurosurgery division at OSU Medical School, Dr. William E. Hunt.

House Staff of the Starling-Loving Hospital, 1941-1942 (Medical Heritage Center, Arthur G. James, MD Collection)

James and his Classmates

More than any other member of the class of 1937, James maintained contact with his classmates, and he served as essentially the permanent organizer of all of their alumni gatherings. The Arthur G. James, M.D. Collection contains many of the responses of former classmates about coming, not coming, remembering, or thanking both James and his wife Millie for arrangements and food, for visits to their home, etc. James often responded after the reunions, rewrote those who failed to come, and praised the arrangements: "The 60th year reunion of the class of 1937 was a huge success. Eleven classmates and eight spouses attended and we certainly had an enjoyable evening of reminiscing. Those of you who could not attend were sincerely missed. Enclosed is a keep sake lapel pin made for the members, and we hope you will wear it with pride." The files include sketches James had helped create for the pins. Vincent and his wife were particularly helpful that year. The invitations, and later reminders to classmates who failed to show up, were also signed by fellow classmates Drs. D. J. Vincent and Trent Smith, and listed the three wives as well. But Vincent said "Art, or really Norma his nurse, did all the work. And don't you ever underestimate how important Millie was to his success."

"Surgery, still the leading method of cancer treatment, has become more efficient, precise and conservative. Alone or combined with radiotherapy and chemotherapy, surgery figures in approximately 70% of the 5-year survivals among cancer patients."
Arthur G. James, M.D.

Chapter 3
Internship and Marriage: the Dreamer becomes a surgeon

Internship Begins

For his first year as an interne (intern was spelled that way then) James was at the Billings Hospital and Clinic in Chicago, a branch of the University of Chicago. This was officially a medical internship, although he already knew he planned to become a surgeon. The decision for a prospective surgeon to begin with an internship in internal medicine was not uncommon in that day, and rotating or mixed internships to prepare young doctors for immediate practice were sought by many. It is possible that Curtis, who had both M.D. and Ph.D. degrees himself, counseled James to get additional training before beginning surgery. Documents saved in the James Collection record that he solidified his interest in cancer during the time he was a young house officer in Chicago, but it was not an easy 12 months. Internship never has been. It is not known what the salary was at Chicago, but Dr. Richard Meiling who served as a surgical intern under Dodd at OSU in 1938, said he was paid $6 per quarter (Sutton).

Interns were called "house staff" because they were expected to be "in the house" at all times. James recalled that the dean "told us we were the property of the hospital for their use at any time. In fact the dean pointed out that if we needed to leave campus for a haircut we should make sure to get permission ahead of time."

Key Mentors in Chicago

While in Chicago, James was particularly impressed by another of his many mentors, the vigorous and literate surgeon, Dr. Alexander Brunschwig (1901-1969) who signed James' diploma after the internship was completed. Brunschwig, the son of immigrants, developed an interest in cancer early in his career, then chose a fellowship in surgical research in France.

Brunschwig received the Lucy Wortham James Medal for his contributions to cancer research in 1962. In 1985 James received the same award for clinical research. Lucy Wortham James (no relation to Arthur) was the great granddaughter of the founder of the first successful ironworks west of the Mississippi River, and the beloved grandniece of R. G. Dun of the financial firm of Dun and Bradstreet. She was beautiful and talented, and although unlucky in love and health this was softened by the fact that she was exceedingly wealthy. She was quite effective in organizing her estate to support several parks and churches, and she endowed the named lecture to honor leaders in the effort to cure cancer.

In 1966 Brunschwig was awarded the James Ewing Medal. In 1967 James was secretary of the James Ewing Society. It is likely it was James who arranged for the award to be given to his former mentor from Chicago.

James' Carolina Connection

From Chicago, James went next to the tobacco town of Durham, North Carolina, and completed a surgical internship at Duke University Hospital. He traveled by train to the new job, and on his first night was assigned to the emergency room. Almost immediately 12 injured patients became his responsibility. In those days no first class medical center supplied significant salary for interns, but he was pleased the board was free and "The food was prepared southern style, and it was terrific" (149/3).

Surgical interns at Duke, James last row, right (Medical Heritage Center, Arthur G. James, MD Collection)

After Duke he returned to OSU for two more years as resident physician in surgery, and the third year he served as chief resident. At OSU the salary was $25 per month, raised to the munificent sum of $100 when he became chief resident, but his life belonged to the hospital and there was not much time to spend money anyway. All of the better surgical programs were designed as a "pyramid" then, and to be chosen chief resident not only meant a chance for more training, but proof that the attending physicians felt you were the cream of the crop. Not all of the young men in such surgical programs, and men they all were, stayed for such additional training.

Mildred Cameron

By his junior year in medical school James met Mildred Cameron. During the two internship years she visited him in Chicago and Durham (191/2). He would surely list that personal tie as the one that truly binds. Mildred's family owned the Cameron College of Cosmetology, and Lillian James, sister of Arthur, was a student there. Mildred described an early date with James and her story reveals a bit about each. "Arthur and I, along with a whole group of friends, were enjoying a picnic down by the Scioto River. The weather was warm and I was wearing a summer dress and open-toe shoes. Somehow I cut my foot. Even though several of the young men were medical students, Arthur was the only one with his medical bag along. He cleaned and bandaged the cut, and insisted I go to a doctor and get a tetanus shot. That was typical of Arthur – so conscientious and concerned" (149/3). Hospital policy at the time required that residents be unmarried, and many a student was told: "Medicine is a jealous mistress." The young doctor James, usually a stickler for rules, broke this one, and on Leap Day, February 29, 1940, left town to marry. Arthur Giangiacomo James and Mildred Cameron were married by a justice of the peace in Kentucky, and after they returned the next morning both went back to work before noon.

Charles Pavey, M.D., the obstetrician who delivered the children of Millie and Art James, wrote on October 12, 1987: "Millie was obviously made to order for you and better than any specifications you might have drawn up yourself. I am sure there are no two people who complement each other better than you two." James felt the same and

Mildred Cameron (Courtesy of James Family)

Art and Millie (Medical Heritage Center, Arthur G. James, MD Collection)

recalled, over five decades after the marriage: "The administration wanted to scare the devil out of us with this rule against marriage. But we did not let that stop us. The biggest thing was just the drive to get married. Since February 29th was Leap Day, a day which did not officially exist, we decided it was the perfect day for the ceremony. And yes, I'd make the same decision today."

The young couple moved in with Mildred's family in a house just south of campus. The family life was busy, how could it not be with two vigorous boys, fishing, travel all over the country, and parents who were as loving as Art and Millie. The James Collection abounds with pictures of the two boys. The character of both, and their happy childhood, assured they would remain both helpful and attentive in the difficult last days that Millie and Art were destined to face.

Art and Millie in front of the fireplace at the Cameron's home (Medical Heritage Center, Arthur G. James, MD Collection)

David, Art and Cameron (Medical Heritage Center, Arthur G. James, MD Collection)

David, Art *and Cameron (Medical Heritage Center, Arthur G. James, MD Collection)*

James picking his prized tomatoes (Medical Heritage Center, Arthur G. James, MD Collection)

"We were attached to heavy bombers in England by the North Sea, and for a while they were carrying out 2000 plane raids a day. We'd know when we saw in what shape the planes were returning, how many casualties we'd be getting. We were generally up most of the night."

Arthur G. James, M.D.

Chapter 4
Military: the Dreamer puts on a uniform

James' Cancer Studies are Interrupted

After completing surgical residency at OSU in 1942, James began a fellowship in cancer at Memorial Hospital – known since 1942 as Memorial Sloan-Kettering Cancer Center – in New York City. His training was interrupted six weeks later by World War II. James knew he was going to be called to service, so he asked to join the Duke staff which had already organized the 65th General Hospital Surgical Unit (149/2). Perhaps related to the recent development of the school – Duke had entered its first medical class as recently as 1932 – Duke had the highest percentage of its medical staff in service of any such unit in the war. The 65th was made up almost exclusively of the Duke medical and nursing faculty, residents, staff, and alumni. James knew the OSU College of Medicine had no similar unit at the time – OSU did organize a smaller unit later. In addition, James liked and admired the Duke staff, and so it was logical for him to rejoin the Duke group stationed initially in North Carolina. In retrospect, one wonders if he would have remained at Duke after his internship in Durham had he not already been thinking of Millie back in Columbus.

The War Department had wisely decided for medical care of servicemen to keep existing medical units, ones such as university hospital staffs, intact as a group; but some military orientation was necessary for everyone. The 65th General Hospital was authorized in 1940 and placed on active duty in 1942, with time first for a long orientation at Fort Bragg. After that time there was an even more prolonged postponement of the originally planned transfer to North Africa due to severe dysentery which swept across Fort Bragg. Captain Brown, a surgeon in Major James' unit, was given the job of opening all the outdoor latrines used by the over 100,000 men camping in the wilds around Fort Bragg, part of a research effort to determine what caused the dysentery. For this duty neither the enlisted men nor the doctors stepped forward with enthusiasm. One transport for Europe did leave, but without the men, and some men lost their personal possessions, including an accordion, books, and special pictures, on the ship that went overseas. After a short stay at Fort Devers, New Jersey, the 65th sailed to Scotland in the fall of 1943. According to testimony by Dr. Ivan Brown, later professor of surgery at Duke, due to activity in the military many of the young doctors postponed certification or completion of their training (129/1). James became a diplomat of the American Board of Surgery in 1943 while he was on active duty (145/1). He became a Fellow of the American College of Surgeons in 1948.

To establish their third tent hospital the 65th was moved from Scotland to England and opened their definitive hospital at Redgrave Park in Suffolk, East Anglia. The site was bucolic, at least until the army arrived and a landing strip was constructed for the return of the big planes. The chaplain of the quaint small neighborhood church befriended the men. While serving with the unit for 44 months it is doubtful James, the busy surgeon, had much time to visit the chapel or to overlook the nearby North Sea. He later said that during 23 months of incessant trauma surgery he obtained as much experience as if he had practiced 15 years. Indeed the family understood that even when coming over on the *Queen Mary*, James was called upon to operate in the surgical suite of the great liner. That seems doubtful for the trip over, because the over 10,000 young men on board were healthy and there were dozens of other physicians, but many wounded men came back on the ship when the unit began to be deactivated. James operated on the return voyage on a man with appendicitis. He was again on that once elegant, now converted, troopship, and it was crowded both coming and going. Brown decades later said the: "mess served food around the clock and the men took turns sleeping in the bunks" (129/1). The ship traveled fast enough that it never had to be part of a convoy, but on the way over the ship used a "zig-zag" maneuver to avoid Nazi U-boats.

During the months in England the surgical unit expanded, with more and more use of tents, and eventually became a hospital of 1,456 beds. The 65th treated 17,250 bed patients, and more than 30,000 outpatients. The primary mission was to attend members of the 8th Air Force, a group that ultimately was flying over 2,000 missions per day across Germany. Many of the injuries of the airmen were severe. Most were a result of anti-aircraft fire, exploding shells, or bullets from German planes, and a few airmen were damaged by the minus 60 degree in-flight temperature. Hospital mortality, death rate after returning to England alive, was a remarkably low 0.4%. The staff reported they could guess the magnitude of the problems facing them by how much damage there had been to the wings and propellers of the planes that limped back. The 65th unit also served wounded

Captain James in U.S. Army uniform, later promoted to Major (Medical Heritage Center, Arthur G. James, MD Collection)

soldiers transferred from the front line hospitals in Europe, for this group there was a lot of surgical patching up needed. One of the few orthopedists said he attended 250 fractured legs in one day.

The Raleigh News and Observer on April 26, 1982, quoted James, "We saw some pretty sad things; things that made you mad as hell. I remember seeing one young man – a young man, 18 or so. Some shrapnel had cut his sciatic nerve. That boy was going to be paralyzed the rest of his life….we saw some pretty sad things" (112). More than one serviceman contacted James later to express personal thanks. An airman who had thoracic surgery by James and Colonel Connie Gardner to remove a bit of shrapnel "as large as a Milky Way candy bar," came back to tell his memories at one of the annual reunions of the 65th (112/1).

On May 8, 1989, a GI wrote to thank James: "I was wounded the twentieth of March, 1945, while in combat in Germany near Cologne. At 09:00 of the above date, I received multiple shrapnel wounds in both legs and a shrapnel wound in the chest. I was hospitalized in an evacuation hospital for removal of shrapnel from my legs and ultimately was transferred to the 167th General Hospital in England. It was noted there that I had a pericarditis with effusion. X-ray confirmed the presence of a foreign body in the myocardium. They immediately transferred me to your 65th General Hospital. A thoracotomy was done by you and Dr. Gardner on April 10th, 1945, and a metal fragment was removed from the wall of the right ventricle. I experienced a Code Blue sometime after surgery...

I guess it frightened everybody, but you pulled me through...My nurse, Lt. Myrtle Threkeld, told me I had the best surgeons… Everything turned out all right, and forty years later I am at age 80 and in pretty good health." James was always memorable to his patients as a "hands-on" doctor, and that patient he did remember well.

Officers of the 65th had already gotten to know each other intimately while they spent the tedious months raising tents and marching in humid North Carolina, long before they ever reached northeastern England. In addition, if it is "bonding" for which one is searching, few things are more powerful at building lasting friendship than the operating room or shared medical and military adventures. It was not always pleasant, even back in rural North Carolina, in those months before the airmen began to arrive at the surgical tents in England. Some bored officer, probably not James, while the group was still trapped in the states, carefully packed ample supplies of alcohol and cigarettes into the ovens that were to be shipped with the unit. The ovens went to a different place, however, and at that other somewhere the cache of goodies must have been discovered with much glee.

Life Following the War

As the war in Europe came to an end it seemed possible that duty in the Pacific would soon follow, but eventually the entire terrible war machine ground to its bloody halt. Finally, after 1945, Major James was able to return to the states and for the first time see his son David Arthur James, who had been born in 1943. His father's name in childhood had been Arthur David Giangiacomo. James' unit was commended not only by the U. S. Surgeon General but by General Eisenhower and the commander of the 8th U. S. Air Force, General Carl Spaatz. James had served as surgeon with that unit for the full 44 months, largely in England.

Reunions of the 65th were often attended by the James couple. Several veterans wrote to thank Art for the pictures he sent after the meetings, but of course it was actually Millie who took most of the photographs. On the 50th anniversary, April 6, 1992, Lieutenant

Major James with David (Medical Heritage Center, Arthur G. James, MD Collection)

General M. J. Ryan wrote to the aging docs of yesteryear: "The future was uncertain, the risk of going to war was great, and the comforts of home begged even the brave not to go. Yet you answered freedom's call, and the fighting men and women of the 8th Air Force were made stronger by your strength, safer by your risk, bolder by your presence."

Typical for him, James corresponded all his life with several members of his old unit, and was fond enough of one of the senior surgeons of the 65th Hospital group, Gardner, to fly to Florida for a visit when his military chief turned 90. Gardner wrote on March 5, 1993: "Arthur was always my favorite as a house officer at Duke and was my able right hand man in the 65th General Hospital during WW II, when I valued his abilities and his calm demeanor" (111/7). Author Paulson remembers Gardner, the pleasant former Duke chair of surgery, and is not surprised at this tribute of James from the professor who was mentor for James first during internship, and then when both served with the 65th.

Statue at Duke University Medical Center honoring the 65th Hospital Group (Courtesy of Erik Paulson, MD)

"It wasn't until I got to Sloan–Kettering that I saw first class cancer treatment."

"In 1935 we talked about one cancer patient in five being cured. Now, we are talking about one in three, and the general feeling is that it could be one in two if we could get all developing cancers soon enough."

Arthur G. James, M.D.

Chapter 5
Cancer Training: the Visionary begins to crystallize his dream

Back at Memorial

As an accomplished surgeon and family man, James could have chosen to come back to Columbus as surgeon at what he was told would be $10,000 to $20,000 per year. The salary for a fellow at Memorial was only $200 per month. Young James seems to have truly believed, even then, what he said after retirement: "If I could give some advice to young people starting out I would say, 'attain the best education you possibly can. Once you have chosen your field, stick with it until you have arrived at the top'" (109/12). Therefore, after military service James did return to Memorial Hospital in New York City, to resume his training and continue his dream of curing cancer. Why Memorial, and what was it? Memorial originally evolved from a research effort sponsored by John D. Rockefeller, who made much of his fortune in oil while living in Cleveland. Other major contributors to

Memorial included Charles "Boss" Kettering, Sullivant award winner as an alumnus of OSU, and Alfred P. Sloan. Both men were successful engineers with General Motors following World War I. The two engineers were well aware of the success of "big science," and of the way scientists had worked together to produce the atomic bomb. Kettering and Sloan not only supplied money to Memorial, but shared the conviction that intense and cooperative scientific effort would someday solve cancer. Memorial meshed easily with the dream of James, and was the ideal place to acquire advanced training in cancer. By 1939 Memorial had moved to a larger facility on East 68th Street, the same street James lived on while training as a fellow when his fellowship program was underway (149/2).

There was, just after 1900, discussion in the world press of a primitive form of immunotherapy employing bacterial vaccines, and a second potential therapy appeared with the birth of enthusiasm about the use of radium to cure cancer. James Douglas, a mining engineer whose daughter had died of cancer, gave 375 grams of radium to Memorial, and by 1915 one third of all radium in the world was in the possession of Memorial. The gift is similar to a donation of Kettering's to establish a Radium Hospital in Columbus in 1920, followed by major donations of General Motors stock to OSU. The radium facility became Doctors Hospital in 1938.

James' Mentors at Memorial

Now back at Memorial, James was lucky once again with his mentors. In addition to all other duties, he had the chance to spend four months in the office of Hayes Martin, M.D. James later said: "There is no doubt in my mind that these months spent with Hayes Martin were the most meaningful of my entire postgraduate training period." Martin was the single man who did the most to develop the

Memorial Hospital in New York (Medical Heritage Center, Arthur G. James, MD Collection)

American specialty of surgical oncology of the head and neck, and it is gratifying that James was the one asked to present the Hayes Martin Memorial Lecture in 1974. But Memorial offered a trove of potential mentors in addition to Martin.

When asked for the name of his favorite teacher, James first recalled that he had many excellent ones, then added, "…but the most memorable, and my favorite, was George T. Pack, M.D." Pack was born in Antrim, Ohio, which still had a population of only 1,275 in the year 2000, smaller even than St. Clairsville. Pack was a graduate student at OSU, and, as did James, Pack sought training in multiple places including at Yale University and then at the Curie Foundation of Radium in Paris, before he finished up at Memorial. He was one of few medical men with more consultations and more community

Dr. George Pack, admired mentor at Memorial (Reprinted with permission from the American Journal of Roentgenology)

awards than James. At the time of his death Pack was on the staff of ten New York hospitals, as well as 25 hospitals outside New York City. He was member of 90 medical societies, on the editorial board of seven medical journals, and his group – he, like James, was at times both part of, and yet practiced outside, his base hospital – published records of their 81,000 patients. But James remembered this indefatigable man primarily as his teacher and role model. He wrote:

> I met him when I began a fellowship in cancer surgery in 1942. He was an extremely competent physician whose specialty was oncology but also an extraordinary person and a tremendous teacher. Dr. Pack was totally dedicated to his patients. He utilized every type of treatment available at the time, and may have been one of the first physicians to realize the value of an interdisciplinary approach to cancer, which meant using combinations of surgery, radiation and chemotherapy for treatment of the various types of cancer to achieve the best results for each patient. This approach is used today by all oncologists. He had a brilliant mind and was constantly striving to find new techniques in surgery. He perfected many surgical procedures currently used in cancer surgery. Perhaps more importantly, he was a kind and considerate physician and treated each patient as a friend. He taught the best methods of treatment for cancer but also how to be innovative. In addition, he showed us the value of kindness, gentleness, compassion, and how to treat the entire patient.

Elsewhere James mentioned another reason he may have been grateful to Pack. After Brunschwig suggested James apply to Memorial, James corresponded with Pack, after all both were Ohio natives. James and only seven other doctors were selected from among

Drs. Pack, Doan, and James at the Columbus Club (Medical Heritage Center, Arthur G. James, MD Collection)

about a hundred applicants. Later James and Pack corresponded, and perhaps Pack even offered counsel, as implied in a letter of June 3, 1961:

> I've been very much intrigued by the statement in your letter of a month ago in which you state there are some things going on at the University that I might be interested in. I only hope that it is not to the detriment of the School of Medicine there, because I really feel closer to Ohio State University than I do to Yale, having spent only my senior year at Yale and going there because I was offered an instructorship with a relatively high salary. Having gotten my Baccalaureate Degree at Ohio State and spending my first three years in medicine there, I look to that institution with greater affection than any other medical school with which I have been affiliated.

There were multiple reasons Memorial soon became synonymous with cancer therapy. The mentors and their students were one reason, of course, but the overall character of the place was fundamental to its success, and it did focus consistently on its mission. The hospital was first designed to help those with terminal disease, but soon grew broader and became a national resource for teaching and innovative research. The early attitude of service at Memorial may have inspired James, and surely his mentors on the wards did. James Ewing, M.D. was famous among the pantheon of heroes at Memorial whom James came to admire and then to emulate. Perhaps he even sometimes remembered Ewing's oft repeated statement: "Am I my brother's keeper? Yes, by Jove I am" (125/8). Ewing was chief pathologist of the hospital in 1912, and in 1931 was named its director. Losing his beloved and socially prominent wife early, this scholarly professor, in fact for a time he was the only full time professor at Memorial, became essentially a recluse as he concentrated on diagnosis and treatment of cancer.

The staff at Memorial, and particularly Ewing, recognized the enormous potential of radiation therapy and knew the early European attempts to use radium for cancer control. Ewing insisted his residents and fellows learn all that was known about radium, study its potentials and hazards, and rely on the use of meticulous pathology as the basis of a new multidisciplinary approach to the treatment of cancer. *Time* magazine on January 12, 1931, devoted its front cover to "Cancer Man Ewing." The article stated: "Not many men have received such homage while they were alive and still among the living." Along with Ewing, William Osler was mentioned as one of the few. There are several pseudo covers in the James files with pictures of James as the *Time* Man of the Year, and perhaps the young Arthur James, while still a senior in college, was inspired by that original Ewing cover photograph.

An alumni organization of graduates from Memorial, after approval of "the chief," coalesced in 1941 and named themselves the James Ewing Society. James became the secretary of the group, and president from 1970 to 1971. By 1973 James was in the middle of planning a broadening of that same James Ewing Society. Some alumni of Memorial were eager to limit the group to alumni from Memorial, others, including James, pushed for change to a more openly inclusive society. He rewrote the by-laws, and led the major reorganization. Despite uproar from traditionalists, the former James Ewing Society eventually adopted the name "Society of Surgical Oncology" in 1975. James was its first president. He was either chair or participant on the Committee for Criteria for Membership and the Plan of Organization of that new society, Credentials Committee, Membership Committee, and he soon became responsible for the list of prospective new members. After he was less in the thick of things, but still attending meetings of the group, he became their informal historian in 1988.

When he came back to Columbus, James was confident he was particularly capable of performing surgery in the head and neck region, in large degree because of the extra training he had received at Memorial from Hayes Martin. Martin, called by some at Memorial "the father of modern head and neck tumor surgery," was the man who had originally formed the Society of Head and Neck Surgeons in 1954. The purpose of the society was to: "exchange and advance scientific knowledge relevant to surgery of the head and neck tumors, exclusive of brain surgery, with particular reference to problems of cancer" (58). From 1967 to 1968 James was president of that group.

In 1958, a somewhat competitive group called the American Society for Head and Neck Surgery was formed, that later became the American Head and Neck Society. Through the years this group included several thousand members in the fields of otolaryngology, general surgery, and plastic surgery. Each time a specialty group is formed within medical circles we can be sure there will be discussion, a tendency to split, and eventually a redefinition of roles. And, of course, any such specialty group, even when it begins from within those practicing in the field, usually moves toward education, research, fund raising, a national meeting, and may empower itself to establish the credentials necessary to be classed an expert. In 1998, and with James no longer actively involved, even though he surely would have been in the midst of it had he been 20 years younger, the merger of the American Society for Head and Neck Surgery and the Society of Head and Neck Surgeons produced the current American Head and Neck Society.

Complexity of Organizations

Now more than a hundred various national and international organizations related to cancer pop up on the internet, a dramatic change from when James began to train at Memorial. Such a plethora of groups with similar goals was already a factor in the mid-portion of his career, and to help solve that problem he helped establish the American Federation of Clinical Oncologic Societies, and became the first President of that group in 1973-1974. A decade later, members of that society began a journal, another accomplishment many such societies yearn to initiate, and the journal continues successfully even now as the *Journal of Clinical Oncology*.

Understanding the complexity of the organizations above is not required to understand James, but the proliferation of groups does imply a medical issue, one that is still relevant. Borderlines between traditional specialties are not given by God, are subject to negotiation, and can lead to disagreements. Does the thoracic surgeon operate on a lump at the base of the neck, or is it the province of a general surgeon or of an oncologist? Is it only the otolaryngologist who is allowed to approach the larynx, or is that region open to some other specialist, one such as a pulmonologist? Even between oral surgeons and oncology surgeons, who should operate on a tumor of the tongue? And the list of overlapping areas can go on and on. James was a cancer surgeon, others with different training felt they could do equally as well. We offer one obvious example from the time James was in his busy years of practice.

William Saunders, M.D., one of the longest serving and most respected physician-chairs at OSU, became chairman of the Department of Otolaryngology in 1961 and served until 1989. When he arrived James was already on the scene, with a robust private head and neck surgical practice. Saunders, but not James, was responsible to teach the residents and specialty fellows otolaryngology, but the clinical material and surgical experience was not readily available to offer to them. James already had most of the patients. Even other ENT specialists, men such as the highly successful John Arthur, M.D., often referred patients with tumors to James. Dr. Saunders thus had to take his trainees to various state facilities, mental hospitals, or prison facilities to expose them to the breadth of surgical and diagnostic material needed for the quality program he was building. It took years to reach accommodation, and later some otolaryngology residents did rotate through James' service as part of their training. The two men eventually did retain such mutual respect that James asked Saunders to attend Millie James when she developed hearing problems. Saunders is understandingly proud that one of the men he trained, David Schuller, M.D. became the successor to James as director of the James Cancer Hospital. There is ample proof in the correspondence that James was equally pleased this otolaryngologist, Schuller, was so obviously the best man to take over the program they had all built together.

Drs. Doan and Wiseman, founders of modern Department of Internal Medicine (Medical Heritage Center)

Leaders at OSU when James Appeared on the Scene

Robert Zollinger, M.D., (1903-1992) was another leader born in a small place, Millersport, Ohio. It is impossible to ignore the fact that many of the successful and hardworking people mentioned in this narrative proudly claimed humble beginnings. Zollinger graduated from the OSU College of Medicine in 1927, received surgical training under the famous Elliot Cutler, M.D. (1885-1947), in Cleveland and in Boston, and was assistant Professor at Harvard when the war broke out. He served in Europe with Cutler as part of the Harvard based 5th General Hospital, having published with Cutler the *Atlas of Surgical Operations* in 1939. That classic text had undergone seven more editions by 1993. For his services in the war, Zollinger received the Legion of Merit and was decorated with the Chevalier de la Légion d' Honneur. Harvard wanted him back, of course, but Dean Charles Doan, who had been ordered by the federal government not to serve in the military but to stay behind to teach students and preserve the shaky school, was an exceptionally persuasive man. At Doan's insistence, Zollinger returned to OSU in 1946. There he chaired and proceeded to build by force of will what became accepted as the best surgical training program in America.

Dr. Robert Zollinger (Medical Heritage Center)

Zollinger published over 400 papers, and was internationally respected as an editor, master surgeon, exacting teacher, and first class showman. Zollinger with Edwin H. Ellison, M.D. (1918-1970), who was the second full time faculty member in the surgery department, described a syndrome now known as the Zollinger–Ellison Syndrome of a tumor in the pancreas which can lead to an ulcer. Zollinger, like James, served as president of several major national organizations, including the American Surgical Association, and was also president of a group that gave him particular pleasure, the American Rose Society. His devotion to the latter group, and his famous prize winning gourds and never to be forgotten country origins, may account for the last of the four things for which he once said he wanted to be remembered: "teacher, surgeon, soldier, and farmer."

Richard Meiling, M.D. (1908-1984), was also from Ohio. He grew up in Springfield and obtained his medical training not only at Jefferson Medical College in Philadelphia, but at Erlangen and Munich in Germany. His Doctorate of Medicine was awarded with honors from the University of Munich, where he also received a scientific award. He returned to the United States in 1938 as surgical intern at University Hospital in Columbus, with later obstetrical training at both Cleveland and White Cross Hospital – now Riverside Methodist Hospital – in Columbus. His military service in World War II was exceptional. He pioneered air evacuation for the allied armies, and as respected physician and skilled linguist in German he interrogated high ranking German war criminals, including Hermann Goering shortly before Goering committed suicide. Meiling became the first reserve medical officer to obtain the rank of Major General in the Air Force. From 1949 to 1951 he was assistant Secretary of Defense and director of Medical Services, and in 1951 he returned to OSU as associate dean of the medical school. Beginning in 1961, after he had replaced Doan as dean of the OSU College of Medicine, Meiling pioneered computer assisted instruction and allied medical education for physical therapy, nurse anesthetists, etc. He supported what was the first, and for a time the only, medical program in air and space medicine. Exposure to the scientific approach to medicine while he was in Germany prompted Meiling, as he related in an interview with Sutton, to encourage writing and scientific investigation at all levels of the College of Medicine.

Dr. Richard Meiling (Medical Heritage Center)

Meiling's interests were broader than just medicine. His concern with tradition and history prompted him to obtain glass art panels for the school, a grand mosaic for the health sciences library, and an official seal for the College of Medicine. The seal prompted other

Drs. Meiling and Zollinger, dear friends (Medical Heritage Center)

units on campus to develop their own unique symbols. Meiling was president of several groups related to the arts in medicine, and encouraged the study of the humanities within the medical school. He also was very active in the Ohio State Medical Association, and developed OMEN, the Ohio Medical Education Network, the radio and TV series that offered continuing medical education to small hospitals in Ohio and far beyond. Meiling was decisive, organized, and able to surround himself with a superb staff. Some on campus feared his conservatism and his energy in building the medical center, but much of the current "bricks and mortar" remain as his monument. He and Zollinger were close friends, less so he and James.

Charles A. Doan, M.D. (1896-1990), was a different sort of man than these two exceptional surgeons. Born, like James, in a small town in southeastern Ohio, he left during his senior year at Hiram College to

Dr. Charles Doan (Medical Heritage Center)

join the U. S. Army Medical Corps, and during World War I participated in research on the influenza epidemic and on meningitis. After the war, he completed requirements that enabled him to attend Johns Hopkins Medical School, the paragon at the time for research-based medical teaching and patient care. For five more years Doan continued his research at Harvard in the legendary Thorndike Laboratories with Dr. Francis W. Peabody, as famous for his lecture that stated "the secret of the care of the patient is in caring for the patient," as he was for the research he encouraged so well. Doan next studied at the Rockefeller Institute with one of the most outstanding researchers America ever produced, Florence Sabin, M.D. Dean J. H. J. Upham, then dean of the OSU College of Medicine, realized how crucial recruitment was going to be if the College of Medicine was to survive, recognized how able and persuasive Doan was, and persuaded Doan to return to Ohio in 1930. Doan was to be full time, following the pattern at Hopkins, at a time when essentially all the teaching at OSU was done on a voluntary basis by clinicians around Columbus, physicians who supported themselves by their private practice. As director of medical research, then chair of the Department of Internal Medicine, then dean, Doan added to his national image as innovative researcher, and soon acquired both the respect and admiration of academics and of the practicing physicians in Columbus. His was the concept of an enlarged health center, of a new University Hospital (now also known as Doan Hall) and a College of Nursing. He initiated the building of relationships with prominent citizens and members of the legislature for the benefit of the OSU College of Medicine, indeed he persuaded all medical students to appeal directly to their legislators for funding. Walter Frajola, Ph.D., who taught biochemistry for Doan, related participating in exchanges with a prospective donor who wanted to contribute to research. Doan asked the biochemist to offer to the donor three plans of varying cost, $20,000 to $90,000, with details about how the funds would be used. Doan started at the $90,000 level, and was only briefly hesitant and stunned when the man asked for how many years. Doan quickly said three, then perhaps wished for more – shades of James' technique of fund raising four decades later. Doan's research and clinical studies proved humans can exist without a spleen, and that removal of the spleen could actually cure some blood dyscrasias. He achieved international fame as a hematologist, and he was elected president of the American Society of Hematology. Over several decades Doan established a leadership tradition in hematology and medical oncology at OSU, a tradition that was destined to continue for decades after he left Ohio State. He received many awards, including the Annual National Division Award from the American Cancer Society, following nomination by James in 1983.

Dr. Charles Doan presenting "Thank You" awards to supporters of the Columbus Cancer Clinic, with James and unidentified man (Medical Heritage Center, Arthur G. James, MD Collection)

Doan was actually an oncologist in the days before oncology had been clearly identified as a separate discipline within Internal Medicine. His interest in helping individuals with cancer led him to become the medical director of the Columbus Cancer Center, a position he turned over to James in 1953. As physician and researcher Doan is remembered for his insightful clinical observations, even more than for his 250 scientific articles. As dean and director of the OSU Hospitals from 1944 until 1961 he was truly beloved by the students and faculty. He served as primary mentor for two generations of alumni, and can be considered the single most outstanding academic leader at the Medical College just before, during, and immediately after World War II. Doan knew his roots were in Ohio, but he also knew the way medicine and science should develop in Ohio. Through all the uncertainties of the time he always remained a courtly gentleman, proud of his profession, and apparently was never visibly angry, nor was he known to complain. When Meiling became dean and took away Doan's office there was dismay in some, but his love of patient care and his unwillingness to cause ill will led Doan to spend his last professional days serving unobtrusively in the halls of Riverside Methodist Hospital.

Manuel Tzagournis, M.D. was student, junior faculty and then the longest serving associate dean, dean, and vice president for health affairs in the history of the medical school. James was one of his teachers, and the success of James is intertwined with their relationship. Tzagournis served in key administrative positions for over twenty years, and continues to be fully active in 2008. Tzagournis was the vice president for health affairs during much of the time James was in the final push for the cancer hospital. Endocrinologist and skillful internist, Tzagournis was, and is, far less flamboyant than was Zollinger, but remains the best known physician in Ohio. He is understated, devoted to OSU and to his patients and family, and a role model in the image of Doan. Like his mentor Doan, Tzagournis established and maintained contact with members of the legislature, often serving as both their personal doctor and as their counselor

Dr. Manuel Tzargournis (Medical Heritage Center)

about medical affairs. Awarded many honors, his contributions included putting to rest the most destructive battle of the medical school, the dispute over the private practice plan. He, more than any other person, shepherded the James Cancer Hospital into an optimal payment system and assured community acceptance. He described arriving very early when still in training and finding James already finishing his rounds.

David Schuller, M.D. should also be specifically mentioned, even though he is not the only significant person who now carries the flag once waved so enthusiastically by James. There are nostalgic linkages to Schuller from names and places that appear elsewhere in this history of James. Schuller replaced James as medical director of the cancer hospital, and followed his footsteps, then enlarged them, as chief development officer. He has published over 250 scientific articles,

James, OSU President Ed Jennings and Dr. Manuel Tzagournis (Courtesy of The OSU Medical Center)

given over a hundred talks about cancer to lay and medical groups, and has excelled in public communications on behalf of the James Cancer Hospital. A Doctor of Medicine graduate in 1970 from OSU, he received additional training in Cleveland, Iowa, and as a fellow with the Pack Medical Foundation in New York. Schuller was appointed chair of the Otolaryngology Department, following William Saunders, M.D., and was awarded the John W. Wolfe Chair in Cancer Research. He has received many honors, but in keeping with what will be mentioned later in this book we note he was the first recipient of the Minton Medal of Honor for cancer research.

These, and other exceptional faculty members we will mention later, were important to James and to the fulfillment of his dream, but by nature he was not really very dependent on others. For much of his career he was more involved with practice and patient care than he was with university personnel, or its politics, but he eventually learned neither of these could be ignored if his dream was to become reality.

Beginnings of James' Surgical Practice in Columbus

James was discharged from the Army in March 1946, completed his training at Memorial from 1946 to 1948, and returned to Columbus and OSU in January 1948. His second son, Cameron, was born to him and Millie on March 8, 1948. His surgical practice began rather modestly after he completed fellowship in cancer surgery at Memorial. In 1948 he was named assistant professor of surgery at the OSU Hospitals, but he was not a full time academician until decades later. He was welcomed back both in Columbus and at OSU, and particularly by Doan and Dodd, but James did not expect a full time faculty position. As we described earlier, there were not many such positions. "Clinical" then, and to a large extent even now, means criteria for promotion depended on service and teaching, rather than on research articles or grants. It also meant, and still does, that any "clinical" individual was expected to be self supporting. He or she could be sure any salary from the hospital, college, or state would be limited. For this reason, and because of what he had experienced with his mentors at Memorial, he expected to return to town as a practitioner of surgery, not primarily as professor in the medical school. It was logical for him to return to Columbus, because both his and his wife's families lived there. Family ties were always fundamental to James. A great opportunity awaited; many doctors had been away and patient needs had been postponed during the great conflict. In addition, James had every right to feel he was better qualified to operate on patients with cancer than any other surgeon practicing in Columbus at that time. After all he was the only one in town who had been recently trained at

Memorial, and, above all, this young doctor never lacked self-confidence or the feeling he could succeed.

For modern readers, particularly anyone in academia, it is hard to realize the extent of voluntary teaching at the time. Central Ohio had been lucky for over a hundred years that practitioners were willing to teach without financial reimbursement. For several generations excellent teaching programs relied on good will and the free contribution of time by some of the most skilled physicians in Columbus. James himself had benefited from practitioners who were informal teachers in Chicago, New York, and at OSU. For years in the community hospitals, and in large degree also at the OSU Hospitals, volunteer teachers were all that was available. James could anticipate joining them. Why did doctors teach, and teach for no money? Practitioners liked the prestige of being labeled academic; a few extra patients came their way because they were teachers; and the apprenticeship system of education still ruled supreme. Idealism also played a role; the title "doctor" can also mean "teacher."

During World War II there was only a skeleton crew to man the medical school, and there was a similarly severe shortage of physicians in the city and in the state. James' medical school classmate, Vincent, who was initially registered to serve as physician in the army, was told it was more important for the war effort that he serve during the war in the small community of Utica, so he did so. Most surgeons were generalists at the time James opened his practice. The same surgeon who took out an appendix might do a leg amputation one day and drainage of a thoracic cyst the next. For some time even the enlightened and dynamic Zollinger resisted moves toward sub-specialization in surgery, as for example even in neurosurgery. He could state, correctly, that as a general surgeon he had performed major brain surgery when he was a junior faculty person at Harvard.

James' Medical Office

James briefly worked along with a medical group downtown, but as soon as possible, by 1949, he bought a house at 1607 Neil Avenue which he transformed into an office. It was at the site now occupied by the OSU College of Nursing's Newton Hall (JC 19). He wrote on September 3, 1954, when he borrowed an additional $25,000 to prepare for an x-ray unit: "With the expanding medical center nearby I am sure this office will always be in demand and that the property will continue to appreciate" (125/22). For personal housing the James family bought a modest home at 2253 Fairfax Road, close to the home of Millie's parents. The family later moved to 1911 Waltham in Upper Arlington, but much of James' effort, and the bulk of his time, was soon spent either at his office at the corner of Neil and 10th Avenue, or in the operating room. Before he began to use the office he

First office building, 1607 Neil Avenue, now the location of the OSU College of Nursing (Medical Heritage Center, Arthur G. James, MD Collection)

remodeled it to include eight efficiency apartments on the upper floors, and nurses often rented these. The office included several examination rooms, and by 1959 was also the location for a radiation therapy unit (119/31, 125/22). Although he did have a radiation technologist in the office, she often served in other capacities as well. His colleague and friend, former chair of the Department of Radiology A. J. Christoforidis, M.D., stated in 2008 that some officials at the university were unhappy that a competing x-ray therapy unit opened up right across the street from the location of University Hospital's efforts using the same treatment modality. But James' radiation unit was not a powerful one; according to Norma Flesher, R.N. it was a 200 KV machine.

James learned at Memorial that all cancer patients could benefit from a multidisciplinary approach, and so he insisted on the same for his patients. Certainly Memorial had been a center for radiation therapy, and fellows in training, including James, were educated in the effects, benefits, and hazards of radiation. The radiation unit at 1607 Neil Avenue was convenient for patients, and might well have paid for itself as well (125/22). Having equipment he could personally control also meshed with his meticulous approach to patient care. Reinhard Gahbauer, M.D., chief of radiation oncology, stated decades later that James was one of only two faculty members who invariably came down to check on their patients while they received radiation therapy. The other particularly meticulous oncologist was Bertha Borouncle, M.D.

The end of the story about the office is interesting, but for the owner was probably disconcerting. Eventually the University did want that parcel of land, as James had foreseen they would. He resisted the original offers. According to his sons, when he was told he must agree or the issue would go to court, and that the legal decision in the case might well be in favor of OSU, James agreed to sell the facility for the benefit of his alma mater. He listed his losses in the transaction after he finally sold the facility in December 1965, as $159,500, and wrote he had sold only "to accommodate OSU expansion with no additional benefit to me" (145/8). Perhaps so, but he did tend to land on his feet.

The Office Staff of James

As was anticipated previously, there is a thread throughout James' professional life from before he left the Neil Avenue office and up until his death, a golden thread that is hard to pin down to any one place in this story. That golden thread is Norma Flesher, R.N., who was trained at St. Francis General Hospital in Pittsburgh before she came to Columbus and began serving on the wards at OSU Hospitals. Norma, as she is called by all, preferred office work to the shifting hours and varied duties of the wards and began working for James in 1959. She served as his office nurse, not as an operating assistant, and her organizational skills were immediately apparent to this man who was himself so well organized.

Very soon Norma was more than executive secretary, office nurse, or just a reliable business manager. She accompanied James on rounds, and Dr. Mike Mishkind, remembering his days as an intern at OSU Hospitals, said Norma would hand James the chart before going into the room, mention the name of the husband, the date the surgery had occurred, and even remind him of new puppies the family had acquired. "The visit by Dr. James might only last five minutes, but to the patient it could seem like a half hour. It was said he would never operate unless Norma was in town." Of course the truth is that she was essentially always in town.

Norma monitored his tight schedule, communicated to patients, stroked prospective donors, and linked the office to national

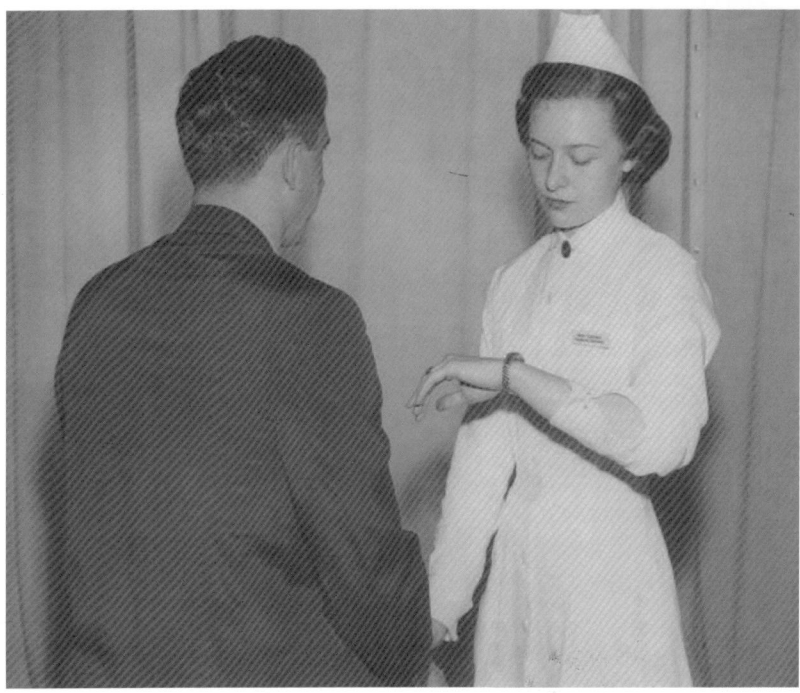

Norma Flesher, RN (Courtesy of Norma Flesher, RN)

executives. After 1982 she also did much of the typing, and there was a lot of it to do. She could pre-assess problems with patients, have a chart review in hand for James, and prepare the note cards James used for his many talks. Essentially every faculty member who has been consulted about how James functioned mentioned Norma as the key to it all. She is modest to the point of being self effacing, quietly humorous, loyal beyond measure, kind to the frightened and calming to the troubled. Her dignity, propriety, and competence are a reminder of the type of selfless service nuns of an earlier generation might have offered to the sick and to those in pain. She would clearly prefer we write less than even these words about her, but James would probably have encouraged even more praise for his nurse colleague of four decades.

His Office after Neil Avenue

In 1965 James purchased a largely unused building at 3100 Olentangy River Road, and he moved his base there in December of that year. This office also needed renovation. It had been an insurance office originally, never designed to house physicians. As before, at Neil, James modified the facility at Olentangy River Road in order that portions could be rented out to others and thereby helped cover the expenses of the building. The building had three floors, and the occupants included dentists, a cardiologist, and a podiatrist. A few simple procedures, surgical follow-ups, and many consultations took place in that office which he used until the mid 1970s. He moved the popular aquarium from the Neil Office to the new one and that simple distraction diverted many who waited anxiously.

Office on Olentangy River Road (Courtesy of James family)

Particularly important at that time in his professional life he had a regular partner, the most significant one of his early career. Joseph A. Bonta, M.D., had been a fine surgical resident at OSU, and was encouraged by James to go to Memorial for a fellowship. The two men worked as partners for over 15 years. Bonta's style was different than James', more overtly sparkly at times, and he was, and always

Joseph A. Bonta, MD, partner of James (Courtesy of Norma Flesher, RN)

remained, a highly respected surgeon. The partnership dissolved amicably when James was spending over half his time traveling for the American Cancer Society. James recommended Bonta for membership in the Society of Surgical Oncology, and for years the two men were considered the leading surgical oncologists in central Ohio. For several years in the 1960s James had another partner, David L. Kinsey, M.D. (123/8), a surgeon and former student who died very young of cardiac disease (115/16). The partnership of Bonta and James was busy enough, but this was a time less was possible to do than is true now, and surgeons who specialized in only cancer were rare. There is one letter in the files in which James counsels a prospective new partner that Bonta was not as busy as he would like to be, and that the prospective new associate had best look somewhere else than in Columbus.

Eventually Bonta gravitated to more full time private practice at Riverside Methodist Hospital (RMH), at the time when it was becoming harder and harder for any doctor to attend patients in multiple hospitals. Criteria for staff privileges had become more stringent, and referral patterns became limited to reciprocal relationships between physicians within the hospital walls, not associations from all over town. This was a logical development as specialists in all areas became common in all the excellent hospitals of the city. For years James operated in any of several hospitals in Columbus, Ohio.

It was suggested by several who were interviewed that James was criticized by some at the University for practicing at RMH, at Mt. Carmel, even at Children's Hospital, while at the same time listing himself as professor at the OSU Medical Center. But he needed an office as well as a chance to get into operating rooms, and OSU assigned him no such office. According to the chair of the Department of Surgery, Dr. Larry Carey, OSU Hospitals at the time sometimes made using the operating rooms awkward and unpredictable. James had solved the problem of an office in his typical fashion. He made a good financial investment with a chance to turn it into something of even greater value. Similarly, he never gave up on doing surgery at the medical school but did use whatever operating rooms in town seemed to work best for the individual patient.

James, in 1961, was turned down for continued clinical practice as a surgeon at RMH, primarily because of his inability to participate sufficiently in staff duties (108/7). Later, at a time OSU Hospitals were in a crunch and unable to supply adequate operating room time for surgeons, he was told by the administrators of St. Ann's Hospital that:

"We will be able to alleviate some of your problems in scheduling operations" (112/1). Nevertheless he rarely operated there. In November 1986, he asked the credentials committee at Riverside Hospital to class him as honorary rather than consulting staff, which meant he lost privileges to practice at RMH. He had already resigned from the staff of Children's Hospital in 1976, again probably because he was too busy.

The land just north of the office that the surgical partnership shared on Olentangy River Road was owned by James. That parcel of land had previously functioned as a landfill. The area was really only a rather trashy hollow, and James and others encouraged companies and individuals to deposit clean fill dirt in the area. Drainage of the large lot became a problem, however, since a 51 inch pipe placed by the city stopped before the river edge was met, and water regularly spilled out onto the open area when it rained. James, at his own expense, extended the pipe to the Olentangy River and then filed and won a lawsuit before the city took responsibility.

There had long been discussion of building a hotel or motel that the family of any patient could occupy while the patient was undergoing treatment. Efforts to get a Holiday Inn placed into that area were not successful. That franchise opened a unit on Lane Avenue. Finally a Hilton Hotel with 232 beds was developed by James with a former American Cancer Society associate from Cleveland, Joseph Silber. In the years to follow, both Len Immke (1923-1991) and David Thomas (1932-2002) would join as hotel investors and the three facilitated turning over the hotel to OSU. Eventually a Ramada Inn franchise occupied the facility that offered special assistance to the needs of those being treated at OSU. Arrangements made it possible to transport the patients or family directly to the medical complex and for years the hotel served as one of the major places for overnight stay of patients and their family.

"The greatest hope for the control of cancer at this time lies in well thought out, well organized, sufficiently funded and properly educated cancer research."

Arthur G. James, M.D.

Chapter 7
OSU and James: Relationships with the OSU Academic Program

The Local Surgeon Becomes Part of OSU

When James began his surgical practice, academic medicine ranged in America from the scientifically oriented full time staff at Johns Hopkins to apprenticeship type schools with no more than two or three full time faculty. In Columbus there were scholarly teachers in the community hospitals. Some of those teachers loved teaching and did it well, but most wrote no scientific articles and achieved no national fame for their hospital. Many of the physicians located at OSU supported themselves full time by care of private patients, and at both OSU and in the community hospitals teachers of the practice of medicine were expected to volunteer time. At the same time there was increasing effort at OSU to limit clinically oriented physicians to those who did all their practice, certainly all their in-patient practice, within the halls of the University Hospitals.

With a foot in the Cancer Clinic, identification at times with RMH, and a busy office away from the University complex, James' widespread style of practice slowly became an anachronism. Gradually more physicians became full time and linked to a single hospital, but administrators still preferred not to pay any of the surgeons, even those 100% at OSU, significant salary. Indeed even in 1973 James' salary from the University had only reached $2,934, for 15% time, but considering the time he was involved in teaching or in resident supervision he was at OSU much more than that (145/7).

James teaching. Although he regularly taught courses at OSU, he talked equally often to numerous groups in town (Medical Heritage Center, Arthur G. James, MD Collection)

Perhaps it did not come as much of a surprise to him, but after James wrote on January 24, 1976 of the need to build a cancer/oncology program in surgery at OSU, the chair of the department, Larry Carey, M.D., wrote him on March 8, 1976, that although he cherished the teaching of James, and although he recognized his current salary was only a token, due to financial stresses even that salary was going to be eliminated. Remarkably, less than a year later, on January 10, 1977, Carey offered James a full time appointment at $26,000 per year, a tenured position as professor, and the assignment to build a separate oncology division within the Surgery Department at OSU. In the last sentence of his acceptance letter of January 24, 1977, James wrote: "I will continue to work for a cancer hospital which I believe would be a strong plus for this area."

Carey, in personal comments to author Paulson, reported failure to recruit other oncology surgeons who matched the local and national stature of James. According to Carey, both Zollinger and Meiling, officially retired, vigorously protested the appointment of James to the full time staff. James accepted the position – never any lack of grace there – and by September 21, 1978 he could report the newly formed Oncology Division of the Department of Surgery had been awarded the first fellowship in oncology ever given by the Surgical Society of Oncology (108/7). William Farrar, M.D., was appointed the first fellow in the new program. Even earlier, on March 29, 1978, Carey had already written Dean Henry Cramblett, M.D., that he looked forward to helping build a cancer hospital at OSU.

After James became full time for the first time in 1977, thanks to Carey, and began operating almost exclusively at OSU Hospitals, administrative duties and time commitment for fellowships, grants, curriculum, fund raising for development, and University committee meetings increased. He continued to remain active in national groups and their boards. Around this time he complained he was "board to death" (116/21). He seemed to have fit into the surgery department well, however, sharing teaching duties, and was probably too busy to note troubles around him, if there were any. Carey was chair of the Department of Surgery from 1975 to 1986 and was succeeded by Olga Jonasson, M.D., the first woman chair of surgery in a major American medical school. The vigorous Zollinger continued on the scene, and he still threw a long shadow. Aware of the new precedent in hiring a woman surgeon, James wrote: "…will there be political hassles, and will Zollie support her" (108/28)?

Chair of Department of Surgery, Dr. Larry Carey and his wife Christine (left) with James at an OSU function (Medical Heritage Center, Arthur G. James, MD Collection)

"As you know, we were not successful in developing the Foundation in cooperation with the Ohio State University. We would now like to establish a Cancer Foundation wholly by the Columbus Cancer Clinic to accomplish the construction of a cancer hospital in this area."

Arthur G. James, M.D.

Chapter 8
Columbus Cancer Clinic: the Dreamer joins and soon leads organizations that fight cancer

The Columbus Cancer Clinic

James' life cannot be parceled out in little bits, or into small fragments. It was a whole tapestry, one woven together by his single minded fight to cure cancer. The story is seamless and almost every day involved his grand quest to cure cancer, and its more realistic corollary, building a cancer hospital for central Ohio. One place to start that part of the James story is with the Columbus Cancer Clinic. But for convenience the local efforts, the national efforts, the research efforts, and the administrative efforts will be discussed separately.

The Columbus Cancer Clinic (CCC) began in 1921, established by Drs. J. F. Baldwin and Andre Crotti. This was the first such free clinic in the capital city and probably the first free clinic anywhere in the nation for detection, diagnosis, and treatment of cancer. At the time many people with cancer were diagnosed late and treated poorly. As James said many times in his career, in 1930 only one out of five persons with cancer could expect a cure. During his later life he could say it had changed to one out of three, then one out of two. When the clinic began there were many people with swollen necks in Columbus, and Ohio was famous for the frequency of goiters. Equally relevant, local surgeons, and particularly Baldwin and Crotti, had developed the ability to remove large thyroid tumors successfully. Crotti had special training in Switzerland, another place with frequent goiters, and the remarkable Baldwin was always sure he could operate on anyone. Crotti was given the first ever Distinguished Service Award from the American Thyroid Association in 1951. That tradition continued in Columbus for a long time, and Ernest Mazzaferri, M.D., expert in thyroid disease and chair of the Department of Internal Medicine, received a similar award in 1999.

The two physician founders actually turned over the issue of fund raising for the clinic to one of the truly heroic women of Columbus, Carrie Nelson Black. According to Mrs. Alice Paugh, herself associated with the clinic for over 40 years, Black once organized a Tuberculosis Society and was one of the founders of what continues as the LifeCare Alliance. Apparently no one could stand in Black's way for long, and she insisted to all that joining in the effort to control cancer was a civic duty. It is hard to accept now, but at the time most women would not even dare say the dreaded word, "cancer." Black was the person chosen by the governor to represent Ohio in Washington at the celebration when Mother's Day became official. The clinic she, as much as anyone, initiated, met weekly downtown at 221 East State Street, near the major medical center of the time, Grant Hospital, the hospital founded by Baldwin in 1900. Baldwin wrote extensively about cancer, devised special surgical approaches, and wrote frequently of his pride in the Columbus Free Clinic, open to anyone regardless of ability to pay. Baldwin died in 1936, but by then Doan was on the scene and was the medical leader at the clinic.

Doan and James' Involvement in the Columbus Cancer Clinic

Doan had particular interest in blood disorders and had developed new techniques to study them. He was a superb and exceptionally responsive internist and even while he was dean of the OSU College of Medicine he continued to volunteer as the medical director of the clinic. In 1923 the CCC had affiliated with the predecessor of what eventually became the United Way, and its own community involvement actually began even earlier with a public awareness campaign, "Are You in Danger?" By Doan's time, in the 1930s, the programs in the clinic already went beyond just screening and diagnosis, and offered expanded services which included home care of cancer patients. Initially some of the outpatient and home services had been located at 330 East Broad Street.

Under Doan's leadership the diagnostic aspect of the clinic moved to the first floor in the North Wing area of University Hospital, the hospital Doan had done so much to obtain in 1951. The location must have seemed convenient, even ideal, to Doan. The North Wing location of the screening clinic was in the unit now named Doan Hall, and had the advantage of being clearly part of the Medical Center and close to the offices of Doan. His office was then in Kinsman Hall, about where the John A. Prior Health Sciences Library is now located.

Soon the Columbus Cancer Clinic was urged to move out of University Hospitals, probably by Meiling. Meiling had assumed many decisions about space within the medical complex. Indeed the official summary of the years of University President Harold Enarson suggests that later Meiling "…was considered by many to be almost as powerful a figure as President Fawcett" (Underwood 163). The follow-up story of the Columbus Cancer Clinic deserves relating, and increasingly involved James, but first, why was there such brief direct linkage to the Medical Center when the clinic was within the halls of University Hospital? The move out of the walls of the hospital involved personalities as well as space.

The change in location of the clinic occurred in 1971 (106/22). Zollinger, it was related by several, wanted that space in the North Wing for other purposes as his department began to expand. It is also true that he was never very sympathetic to the establishment of a separate oncology clinical service. At the time many chairmen feared "Balkanization," splitting up of surgical areas into autonomous pieces. Space was tight, as it always is, and particularly space adaptable for research. The almost moribund OSU College of Medicine was becoming awake, larger, more research oriented, and more clearly identified as distinct from competing practice groups in Columbus. Again we must look back at the times. The current OSU clinic building designed for patient care and teaching, and now named Cramblett Hall, did not become available until after 1974. But personalities often matter in major decisions about space.

Carey and others have commented on the friendship of Zollinger and Meiling, and of their ability to work cooperatively for the benefit of the College of Medicine. The two surgeons shared much. Meiling and Zollinger reveled in their experience in the military. Zollinger had received medals for his military service as a surgeon, and Meiling kept his flag as a two-star general of the Air Force beside his desk. Meiling was disciplined and well organized, and his extensive political ties in Washington helped the medical school and hospitals obtain funds and launch new programs such as Allied Medicine. Zollinger was building a new surgical program and a major national image. Doan had not shared in overseas service; he had been back in Columbus holding the school together during the war. After the war, James, who had served well but rarely mentioned it, began to develop as significant a base of community connections, important friends outside University Hospital, as was true of Meiling and Zollinger, both of whom were very successful full time academicians.

It is unlikely the suggestion that the CCC move out of University Hospital in 1971 was intended to be harmful or vindictive to either Doan or to James. The three leaders, Meiling, Zollinger, and James at times later did work fruitfully together. There were multiple considerations that played a role in forcing the move. The clinic was fundamentally a community service, not an academic unit. University Hospitals have never been able to accommodate all community organizations that might request, may even merit, space and financial assistance. How can OSU administrators, save for allowing an occasional lecture or two, accommodate the hundreds of support groups related to medicine and health, groups ranging, perhaps, all the way from Alzheimer's disease to Yaws disease? The current Cramblett Hall has managed for years to house a unit related to the Lions Clubs of America, the eye bank, but this offers a linkage program for those needing corneal transplants at OSU Hospitals. The area in back of the North Wing of Doan Hall, labeled on an early map (page 265 in Vol. 3 of OSU College of Medicine history) for cancer therapy, in fact did continue to house the radiation therapy area many years later, but it was not illogical to ask Doan and James to move the clinic out of OSU hospitals.

Doan was approaching the tail end of his illustrious career when James came back on the scene as a part time faculty member, and Doan surely welcomed James' enthusiastic participation in the CCC. He may even have suggested James as chair of the cancer committee of the Ohio State Medical Association in 1957. By then, James had been director at the CCC over four years. The two were close friends and the volunteer and later director, Paugh, said it was common to see Drs. James and Doan, perhaps walking along with a favorite orthopedist of the time, Jud Wilson, M.D., with arms linked while in animated and pleasant conversation.

The Dream Creates Disagreement

James, as judged by dozens of letters and reported conversations in the mid 1950s and early 1960s, spoke openly and often of the need for a free standing cancer hospital. This concept, a free standing hospital like Memorial, did not mesh with the dreams of Zollinger and Meiling for enhancement of the College of Medicine as a whole. Although letters in the files never speak of personal disappointment or pique, it is possible James perceived the required move out of the university area as a rebuff, as evidence he must look elsewhere than the university to fulfill his dream for a center to combat cancer. On July 18, 1955 he wrote Dr. Howard Berman, Director of the City of Hope Medical Center in California, that he was: "very much interested in any further information you can give me regarding the position you have available." He stated he was associate professor, as well as associate medical director (with Doan) of the CCC. In one list of his curriculum at about the same time he listed himself as "clinical associate professor," but at that time there was not a clear cut designation that matches the current "clinical track." He almost surely meant he was supported largely by clinical activities, rather than with a full time salary.

Is it possible that Zollinger somehow disliked or opposed James? At least seven people who knew both men have said so. No one told these authors that James disliked Zollinger. James nominated Zollinger for several national awards including, on October 27, 1978, for the

General Motors Sloan Cancer Research Award for basic research (110/23). James helped Zollinger with revisions of his textbook of surgery several times, and after they appeared on panels together Zollinger wrote him several gracious thank you notes. There were many overlaps later in their careers, and each knew very well that the other was highly respected locally and nationally.

Among reasons offered by former friends for the reputed antipathy of Zollinger for James are the following: 1) James did much of his work outside University Hospitals and therefore was perceived as less than fully loyal. James' lifetime contributions refute that charge, however. 2) Zollinger was heard by several to complain that James had become "too wealthy." Zollinger's office was notoriously inefficient in billing and collecting. James, from his time working as a boy at the grocery store, was meticulous and scrupulous about debts, and punctual about billing. In addition he invested wisely in the surrounding area, and several of his personal properties did well. 3) James had more patients than Zollinger. 4) According to several people who were interviewed Zollinger once "sanctioned" James for a perceived indiscretion. This is no easier to prove or refute than that Zollinger was envious of the other man's national image and local prestige. Either seems possible, of course, but neither seems totally explanatory, nor relevant, when the lives of these two exceptional men are judged as a whole. They were both too busy to fret overly much about the other. 5) One physician who considered himself a very good friend of James suggested that there was a "quiet" elitism, snobbery, in Columbus, and "Art was a short swarthy Italian who had changed his name." If that hypothesis is considered, it should be placed against what is a certainty: no physician in Columbus was a friend of so many governors, legislators, and influential entrepreneurs, and rarely was a physician so accepted by both his fellow physicians and by the rank and file doctors in his town. In addition there have probably been few other physicians, until perhaps his recent successors including Schuller, who raised more money for the university from friends and patients than did James. And James always had the gift of representing a cause rather than himself.

We suggest another reason for perceived differences, or for antipathy of which in fact there remains little overt evidence. James was quietly serious to the point of seeming unduly dignified, even European. James walked quietly along the side of the hall, Zollinger created a memorable stir wherever he went. As a surgeon who built his own practice, James held onto patient loyalty, administrative positions, and duties that others might have envied, indeed sometimes did envy. There are always some who envy a successful man or woman. And, above all else, James was after a totally new hospital. That was unequivocally perceived as unwise, even as a threat, by many physicians and academics in Columbus.

This discussion is already prolonged to the point of near unseemliness, but we must remember these two men were among the most remarkable, interesting, and successful people who ever served in Columbus. Physicians then, and now, did not all agree with James about the hospital, its autonomy, its independence, or even the need for it. The most useful summary about those now distant days may be that supplied in 2008 by E. Christopher Ellison, M.D., vice dean of clinical affairs, and the current Robert Zollinger Professor and Chair of Surgery. His parents were "long-time family friends" of Millie and Art James. Ellison describes James as a "consummate gentleman" and an "outstanding role model." He adds: "I think his and Zollinger's relationship was complicated in many regards. James wanted to build a free-standing hospital; however, I am not sure if Zollinger was in favor of that or not. We did have a surprise party for Dr. Larry Carey when he left Columbus to go to the University of South Florida, and James and Zollinger came to that party. I clearly remember them walking out arm-in-arm supporting each other when the party was over. That is a fond memory I have of both of them together, and I think if there was any angst in their relationship, it was put aside for the betterment of the institution during those many years."

Aside from the obvious potential linkage between a man who was interested in cancer and a designated cancer clinic, what attracted James to devote time, at no recompense, to the indigent population of the CCC? For one thing there were humanitarian concerns, and he was able to recruit other similarly idealistic physicians in that day before medicine became a business. The year end report in 1959 for the CCC, and year end reports for decades after, lists James as medical director, but he is never alone (56/1). Thirty five attending physicians, including leading doctors in Columbus, were listed as volunteer physicians at the clinic. Many of these had been former students and had come to share his antipathy to cancer. In several reports of the clinic, Zollinger was specifically praised in James' summary of progress in cancer surgery in Columbus.

Another reason for the interest of James in the clinic was that he grasped the possibility of using the clinic as a stepping stone to the hospital he envisioned. Already on November 29, 1954, a resolution had been passed that the board of directors of the CCC appoint a committee of not less than seven to establish a facility to provide inpatient care for cancer patients. On September 26, 1957, a hospital fund of $100,000 was established with monies from prior memorial contributions. By 1961, a firm considered expert in fund raising was consulted, and on March 3, 1962, *The Columbus Dispatch* reported: "The Columbus Cancer Clinic hopes to build a $2.5 million, 100 bed hospital in Columbus" (JC 150).

Columbus Cancer Clinic History

The CCC, always in the past and even now, remained a clinic for the care of the indigent population, but was never limited to that group alone, nor was it limited to any one specialty. The keys to continued success of the CCC included its selfless service and sustained focus on cancer. In 1970 the clinic moved into its larger facility at 550 Thomas Lane, finally in a place well able to house all of its programs. It was essentially on the Riverside Methodist Hospital (RMH) campus in a building still in use, now by the Riverside Human Relations Office. Indeed at about that time James discussed buying additional land just north of the hospital, on the west side of Olentangy River Road, and hoped to use that as a location for a hospital to replace the clinic. This would have been about where the original Kobacher Hospice was located.

James speaking at dedication of Columbus Cancer Clinic building, Doan to his right (Medical Heritage Center, Arthur G. James, MD Collection)

That building is now the current Human Resources building at Riverside Hospital (Courtesy of George Paulson, MD)

James wrote to Edgar Mansfield, Chief Executive of Riverside, regarding the feasibility of placing a cancer hospital contiguous to Riverside Hospital, but administratively independent of it. Tentative floor plans and space requirements were addressed, including areas for research. A budget of $2.5 million dollars was suggested.

When administrators at Riverside Hospital bought the building on Thomas Lane from the CCC, the clinic purchased from the Ceramic Society the current CCC facility at 65 Ceramic Drive, near Whetstone Park of Roses. After the clinic moved to Ceramic Drive in 1987 it continued its previous roles, but times were changing. A program was given the name "Rays" to symbolize outreach, sunbeam rays of hope, and one note says the program was initiated to honor a cherished nurse, Mary Scarlett. Rays was established in 1946 to raise money through the efforts of volunteers in local neighborhoods. Individual support groups would be the "Rays" of a community, a church, or a neighborhood, and there was a yearly fellowship banquet to enhance sharing of resources. One of the leaders in the Ray program was Fran Gumble, sister of the esteemed Rabbi Folkman and thus aunt of the famous Harvard scientist, Judah Folkman, M.D., whom James twice hosted at OSU. She may have encouraged the Hadassah Myrtle Wreath Award given on March 19, 1974, to James. The "Rays," the Board of Directors of CCC, and the hundreds of devoted volunteer workers were even more important in raising public awareness of cancer than was the several million dollars the CCC eventually contributed toward realization of the hospital.

It was soon apparent that the clinic was never going to raise enough money to fulfill what it saw as its duties, even with the help of all the Ray groups combined. Over 500 individuals with cancer arrived at the clinic each year, and they needed an ever widening range of assistance. Services included medical supplies, wigs and prostheses, equipment, transportation, even food. A successful mammography program was launched. In 1994 home care originating from the clinic could be certified by Medicare. Despite this potential for improved financial help, and all the volunteer efforts, the monetary pressures steadily grew.

The Future of the Columbus Cancer Clinic

Hospitals all over the county do continue to refer indigent people with cancer to the clinic, there remains little enthusiasm in most other facilities to care for those with no funds. Noting its shrinking endowment, the CCC joined LifeCare Alliance in 2005, and will eventually move from its location on Ceramic Drive. LifeCare Alliance is a praiseworthy local organization that is most recognized, perhaps, for its linkage with Meals on Wheels. LifeCare Alliance is involved with Visiting Nurse programs, also founded by Carrie Black, and other initiatives that mesh well with the modern attempts of the CCC to be involved with home care support. Diagnosis is now usually accomplished in other venues. The basic policy of the clinic, to supply indigent care, absolutely continues. No one is eligible for the numerous services unless they have active cancer and an income less than 150% of federal poverty guidelines. Until the late 1980s chemotherapy was being administered in the clinic, but the science of chemotherapy began to require a more complete program than most free standing clinics could expect to supervise. Earlier the costs of the chemotherapy program were covered in part by White Castle and members of the Ingram family who have been one of several multigenerational supporters of CCC. In addition to all else, the decades of single minded devotion of experts like Doan, James, and William Farrar, M.D., was never going to be easy to replace.

There has been steady evolution in Columbus from the days Crotti or Baldwin would palpate a goiter and decide regarding surgery, up to modern times with outpatient services never contemplated when James began his career. He insisted, always, that something could be done for any patient in need, and even in the terminal phases of cancer help could still be offered. He was not very enthusiastic, however, about having a hospice program within the hospital itself, fearful that would weaken efforts to cure or ameliorate. Warren Wheeler, M.D., who led in the establishment of the first hospice in Columbus, and who began the administration of chemotherapy at the clinic, wrote in 2008 that James was so eager to push for a cure that he did not recognize some of the terminal care initiatives which are now common. Furthermore, the early chemotherapeutic agents were less effective than those available now, and James was a surgeon and a man searching for a cure, not for palliation. Ivan Gilbert, M.D., stated, however, that James sent him to Canada to learn about the hospice program there, and in the correspondence files James rejoiced when Constantine Benedetti, M.D., joined OSU to assist with pain management and palliative medicine. James would not be surprised that one of his most trusted colleagues, the popular Farrar, serves as the current Medical Director for the CCC. Indeed James probably engineered it. The couple had been friends for years and James greatly respected Farrar.

Mrs. Kathryn Farrar and Dr. William Farrar with Millie and Art (Medical Heritage Center, Arthur G. James, MD Collection)

James' Involvement in Other Community Groups

One can wonder, of course, if the very success of the James Cancer Hospital, and that of other hospital programs in the Columbus area, increased awareness in the community of the need for long time care, hospice care, palliative care, and neighborly support for those who are not cured but who despite cancer can continue a meaningful life. Cancer is not always the death sentence it once was considered. The efforts of the clinic, the clinic so contributed to by James in leadership and fund raising, and then led by Farrar more recently, is part of the reason. James' service from 1954-1989, thirty-five years as medical director, is similar to what we will see in all his professional and service activities. He did not drop out of a position from boredom or frustration, never relinquished a needed service or potentially useful position, nor fatigued in his commitments. He used his professional skills to treat those in need, lead organizations, link wealthy potential donors (often prior patients) to the goals of the program, and then helped lead planning to assure solving problems at hand would enhance long term goals.

His desire for community involvement, and his lifetime thrust to educate, diagnose, and cure cancer led this basically shy man to visit, or join, many groups in town. Soon he was busy talking at county medical meetings, to luncheon groups, to leagues of women, all the while inching up his way nationally through both his academic accomplishments and through public service. The James Collection holds hundreds of thank you letters for his participation or advice. The James Collection also preserves some of the cards or notes he used, but he spoke informally even more often. He gave 17 talks in one six-month period in 1990, and more during any similar length of time when he was president of the American Cancer Society. For decades he responded enthusiastically to requests to be the speaker for county medical societies, local civic groups, and service organizations of all sorts. From that perhaps more innocent day there are not many letters suggesting an honorarium was offered, but several times he suggested, as was typical of his friend Coach Woody Hayes, that any payment for his talk should go to charity. The talks were much the same, one can suspect: We have come a long way in cancer therapy, we need more research, and Columbus would benefit from having a hospital devoted exclusively to the treatment and cure of cancer – talks that were simple, repetitive, and effective.

To demonstrate his style of leadership we offer just one example of involvement, a community program in which James was an integral part. Columbus is home to four medical groups. Each includes doctors from various disciplines within medicine, and the members are representative of the staff at several hospitals. Each group meets monthly to review medical advances, socialize, and educate one another. The first group, Medical Review, began in 1928. The official names are: The Medical Review Club of Columbus, Round Table of Medical Arts, The Medical Symposium, and The Columbus Medical Forum. From 1950 until about 1985 membership was considered an honor, but less so recently. There are now many other educational venues and fewer doctors who care to go out at night for a heavy meal and to hear a lecture in a specialty area other than their own, and there is decline in enthusiasm for all such groups. All hospitals have excellent educational programs, and it is easier to get credit for continuing education, a legal requirement, in such larger venues.

James joined the Columbus Medical Forum, and as was his style participated readily with talks and consistent attendance, and soon nominated others for membership. In 1973 alone he nominated Drs. William Inglis, Charles Mattingly, Thomas Mallory, James Blackford, David Kelly, and Herndon Harding. As of 2008, four of these men remain on the role of the group, and as an example of James' wide circle of medical colleagues, only one of the men was identified primarily with OSU Hospitals. In 1965 James was elected president of the group, and his wife arranged the dinner pictured here (80/3).

Columbus Medical Forum Annual Banquet for members and guests (Medical Heritage Center, Arthur G. James, MD Collections, photo by Millie James)

After the cancer hospital was a structural reality, he gave a final talk to the group: "Should members of the Medical Forum send their patients to the Cancer Hospital?" You can guess his answer.

Even in this modest example of a community group, the manner by which James became so influential and a key member of so many groups is apparent. He joined, remained active, corresponded, assumed a committee chairmanship or took lesser roles, and then became the designated, often elected, leader. If he did not have a dream of the potential for himself and for the organization, he did not long remain a member. He joined, but eventually failed to renew membership, in the Columbus Maennerchor, a German singing and social club in south Columbus. He was a charter member of the Columbus Capital Club, but soon dropped his membership, surely because he was not one to sit and chat at lunch in a downtown club, however nice it may have been.

In discussing his memberships and organizational efforts, it is important to reemphasize the role of his beloved Millie. She accompanied him on most of his longer trips and recorded the experience in photographs. She is almost always mentioned in letters of thank you for his services. She softened his busy surgical life, maintained their many friendships, and planned major events. At least four couples interviewed have mentioned that they often enjoyed her hospitality. Some couples maintained a once monthly outing with Art and Millie. Several letters in the collection noted gracious events at the "farm," a prime location for outings with donors as well as friends. It was in large degree Millie, almost no one called her anything else, who maintained the social ties that bound.

"All cancer will eventually be wiped out; there's no doubt about that. I don't know how long it will take... but I am sure the day is coming."

Arthur G. James, M.D.

Chapter 9
American Cancer Society: the Dreamer marches onto the national stage

James' Steps to National Prominence

The American Cancer Society (ACS) consumed more of James' time and energy than any other of the many organizations he contributed to, and may also have been among the most useful for him in assuring the success of his dreams for Columbus. Some of the executives of the time considered him the most effective of the presidents of the ACS (116/9).

James joined the Franklin County Unit of the ACS soon after he arrived back home in Columbus. He was a member of the Board of Directors for the local chapter from 1948 to 1990, and the medical advisor from 1948 to 1979. By 1950 he had become active in the state wide division of ACS, and he remained on that board of directors until 1992. He was president of the Ohio division from 1957 to 1960. These duties, and how he fulfilled them, opened for him a position in the national organization, and by 1963 he was on the national board of directors.

The reader can guess what happened next. His progress is reflected in dozens of letters thanking him for his consistent service. He assumed chairmanship of any committee that requested his help, shaped its activities, and then moved up to another committee. These committees included, just for the national ACS organization: Executive, Medical and Scientific, Professional Education, Public Education, Service, Film, Lay Nominating, Awards, Fellowship, and finally the Crusade Committee. From 1972 to 1973 he was president of the ACS.

As the representative of ACS he had the chance to hobnob with numerous national figures supporting the effort against cancer. Included were Joan Crawford, Lawrence Welk, and Gregory Peck, and surely he smiled to meet Minnie Pearl from the Grand Ole Opry. He also administered an exam of the neck to then Ohio Governor John Gilligan.

Entertainers Lawrence Welk and Minnie Pearl with James (Medical Heritage Center, Arthur G. James, MD Collection)

Actor Gregory Peck with Art and his son Cameron (Medical Heritage Center, Arthur G. James, MD Collection)

James examining Ohio Governor John Gilligan's thyroid (Medical Heritage Center, Arthur G. James, MD Collection)

During his presidential time he was busy and on the road, and it was years, not just one year, because as president-elect, chair of the science and grant awards committee, and later as a member of various boards he fulfilled numerous official duties, trips, or lecture requests. Those years for James meant his respected partner, Bonta, would move on to practice full time at Riverside Hospital. And it meant James would be busy indeed. We must remember during this time he continued to see and operate on patients, serve local groups including the Columbus Cancer Clinic, and he visited with potential donors and friends in the fight against cancer. During his presidential year James chose, on behalf of the ACS, to emphasize not just diagnosis but earlier diagnosis, and renewed his battle against smoking. In 1973 he testified to Congress, wrote dozens of letters and particularly tried to restart lapsed TV advertisements against tobacco. Several of his anti-smoking pronouncements for ACS directed to the press were picked up all over the country and articles appeared that mentioned the effort, and his name, all the way from Portland, Oregon, to Jacksonville, Florida. He attempted to elicit local community and physician activism, and in 1974 he wrote in the *American Journal of Surgery* "How many of us work in hospitals that have cigarette machines available to the patients? Should we condone this in these 'Institutes of Health'" (148/16)? "The greatest accomplishment in cancer prevention is in the development of evidence which conclusively showed that cigarette smoking is the principal cause of lung cancer" (50/6). Through his presentations and the frequent comments about his activities in *The Columbus Dispatch*, the community of Columbus became well aware of his name, of his push for earlier cancer diagnosis, of his campaign against smoking, and, above all, of his dream for a cancer hospital.

All this fit the pattern of his life but never, even in the glory days as the cancer hospital became reality and not just a dream, did James spend so much time in professional travel as he did when he led the ACS. True, the trips to Canada and Alaska did enable him to do a bit of fishing, which he loved; the Japanese trips offered a glimpse of elegance; and, the ones to Indonesia led to lasting friendships. He wrote back to his new friends to order objects he had admired.

Nevertheless, the extensive travel must have been wearing, even if it often was softened by the presence of Millie.

Taj Mahal in India, trip for the American Cancer Society (ACS) (Medical Heritage Center, Arthur G. James, MD Collection)

On canal in Venice, representing the ACS (Medical Heritage Center, Arthur G. James, MD Collection)

James in Mexico, professional trip for ACS and, for once, no necktie (Medical Heritage Center, Arthur G. James, MD Collection)

When James accepted the presidency of the ACS in October 1972, he mentioned the success of mammography, and the thrust for a cure, and that was when he suggested the coming year be named "The Year of Earlier Diagnosis." As president he traveled over 100,000 air miles, visited 23 states, and made official visits to four countries. He was asked to give innumerable talks, symposia, and workshops, and to join panels all around Ohio. In November 1972, he was a keen participant at a National Chemotherapy Conference held by the ACS in New York City, and of course since the time of that conference "chemo" has become even more a mainstay of oncology. Already by the early 1970s at least eleven types of cancer could be suppressed by chemotherapy. Both leukemia and Hodgkin's disease responded well, even dramatically, to proper chemotherapy. He attended a national meeting on the relationship of herpes virus and cervical cancer in December 1972. Exposure to such educational meetings fit well with his earlier education about immunology, and the benefits and hazards of radiation when used for therapy. For the rest of his life James would speak of the possible role of viruses as causes of cancer, of the potential for use of immunological techniques in therapy, and of astounding advances in radiation and chemotherapy. As recently as 2008, and with regard to the brain tumor of Senator Teddy Kennedy, James' old training hospital at Duke in North Carolina reported possible success with an individualized vaccine for therapy of brain tumors.

During his time representing the ACS, James chaired a postgraduate course on cancer in the Dominican Republic with 250 participating physicians. The visit made it possible to assess lay support groups in that country, and he noted the government officially supported such service organizations, in contrast to what was common in the United States. The President of the Dominican Republic hosted the social program, and this and other events outside the scientific conference seemed as memorable as were the formal talks. James met a similarly warm reception in Peru. A Science Writers Seminar in Arizona in March of the presidential year saw James offering one of the keynote addresses. At that time he again made a vigorous statement condemning smoking, including smoking at all such professional meetings. He routinely bemoaned the decline in advertisements against smoking, these having been terminated after all television advertisements for smoking were banned. James offered public challenges to the broadcasting moguls to resume anti-smoking spots on TV. He had no success in this endeavor.

Eight hundred persons attended an International Symposium on cancer detection and prevention, held in Bologna, Italy, April 9-12, 1973. James, as representative of the ACS, met there with his counterparts from Italy, Russia, Cuba, Japan, and several European countries. He was able to explain, and in Italian, the "Seven Danger Signals," to a reporter.

In support of the budget for the National Cancer Institute, James appeared before the Appropriations Committees of the House of Representatives and the Senate in May and July of 1973. He urged Congress to raise the budget to $640 million, rather than the $500 million that was proposed. He made a particularly strong pitch for training grants; these had been taken out of the budget. He explained the need for education in oncology, defined that relatively new discipline, and pushed for more radiotherapists and medical physicists. He reported seven cancer centers were to be identified, with eight more to come, and reviewed for Congress the potential combined efforts of the government and the ACS in establishing these innovative new units for research. One can be sure he was already contemplating having one awarded to OSU, and eventually the OSU Comprehensive Cancer Center did appear.

"The banquet speaker is first subjected to a sumptuous repast — plied with foods delicious and calorie laden — and is expected to arise and before his equally stuffed audience and be brilliant, entertaining, informative, inspiring, and invigorating. I mention this so you won't expect any of these results."

Arthur G. James, M.D.

Chapter 10
Travel as a Mission: trips of the Dreamer

One Role of the ACS Presidency was to Give Talks

James clearly enjoyed the trips to England, and of course particularly the one to Italy, seeing former acquaintances and newer facilities for cancer therapy, but the trip to Greece was particularly memorable (54/12). One of the several hosts in Greece was Dr. Christoforidis, later professor and chair of the Radiology Department at OSU, who was one of the early participants in the radioactive gold seed therapy that James and his friend William G. Myers, M.D., Ph.D., pioneered. James dictated enough about the Greek trip to fill 27 pages about his impressions, and he recorded a great deal about meals and sights along the way. He reviewed head and neck surgery performed by the group in Athens, visited medical institutes, and lectured to students and staff. At the Congress of Dermatology in Greece he presented a lecture on cancer of the thyroid gland, and one on cancer of the head and neck. Since he had written so often about melanoma he participated in that portion of the meeting as well.

Art and Millie in Greece, a trip he particularly enjoyed (Medical Heritage Center, Arthur G. James, MD Collection)

About 20 miles north of Athens he visited two institutions housing patients receiving the basic diagnosis of cancer, centers that coordinated the process of outpatient therapy. He noted with particular interest an institution designed for optimal terminal care. The large cancer hospital in Thessalonici was new in design, planned for 250 patients, and had an area nearby for research. He was struck by the difference in philosophy in dealing with patients; staff doctors in Greece considered it important **not** to tell patients they had cancer. James felt exactly the opposite.

He flew from Greece to London, was impressed there by the nursing facilities for patients, with many of these located in small homes, and he could sense the beginning success of the hospice movement which flowered in England. He wrote of sharing lunch with a member of the House of Lords, of a memorable meal sitting next to the elegant Lady Compton, and of impressive portraits in the Royal College of Surgeons. He saw the anatomical specimens in the Hunterian Museum – all heady stuff for the boy from Belmont County. He also discovered that England lacked anything comparable to the ACS, and in substitute had to rely on the Marie Curie Foundation. He was pleased on the other hand with British rehabilitation programs for cancer patients and wondered if Columbus could someday do as well. In fact, after he returned, the Columbus Cancer Clinic did begin just such a program.

James' Contacts and Comments

In October 1988 in a speech to the Ohio Division of the American Cancer Society James reviewed the early history of cancer, and noted the sense of hopelessness that seemed all pervasive in the early 1900s. He described, with pride, the accomplishments of the Society. He was still bothered by what he heard 15 years earlier, as he said: "I visited several foreign cancer societies in 1972-1973. The feeling as to what should be told cancer patients was quite different from what we are accustomed to. In some places they are very adamant in believing that it is inhumane to tell patients they have cancer. The doctors believed that it was better to let patients go ahead with their illness and even die with it, and at least 'the patients did not have to worry about having cancer.'" He suggested the most important single role of the Society was to educate the public, and that women were the natural leaders in that effort.

There was steady progress in both therapy and in prevention. One of his mentors, Dana Farber, M.D., was praised by James as the first one to cure anyone by the use of chemotherapy. James rejoiced that 300,000 people were being cured each year by such chemotherapy. James mentioned the "Pap Smear" test of George Papanicolaou, and noted the value of a test that saved so many from uterine or cervical cancer. In 1962 Dr. Papanicolaou received the Lucy Wortham James award from the Ewing Society for his efforts in developing the preventive test for uterine and cervical cancer (73/15). After the death of the Greek scientist-physician whom James had admired both in Greece and in America, he arranged for Mrs. Papanicolaou to receive an award from OSU. The regular use of another preventive test for women, mammography, was encouraged by the ACS, and urged enthusiastically locally by James as it became a new service of the CCC.

James, who had been one of several people in charge of both grant awards and the raising of funds, in his address went on to praise the ACS for an increase in the research budget from $1 million dollars in 1946 to $82 million in 1987. Prevention and the role of cigarettes still merited his attention, years after he chose that as a primary focus of the Society. One might assume his talk would end as he says: "With

His interest in combined data began early in his career. His summary efforts were used for decades by specialty groups, and he chaired several local committees to attempt adequate record keeping about what was being accomplished, as well as recording missteps along the way. This effort began in his office, where he and Norma maintained careful registries of patients with cancerous tumors, those with benign tumors, and a record of those patients without cancer but with concern. They developed a detailed coding system to assure follow-up, diagnostic verification, and correct addresses for later reports and billing.

There are dozens of letters, always gentle ones, representing his responses to bizarre inquiries from the public. The topics included "Rand Vaccine" (112/1), serum inoculations, distortion of bones as a potential cause for cancer (109/29), or the potential that dogs cause cancer in humans (108/1). An electromagnetic device appeared in Dayton and was touted as a cure-all, but he reported it was useless. Everyone wanted an answer for his or her particular question, and many offered their theory of causation. The hazard of various vaccines, special diets, or of presumed toxins, could be the subject of an inquiry. And sometimes the letter just recorded a simple request from a school child seeking to write a paper about cancer. Many of the inquiries were channeled to him when he was president of the ACS, or followed one of the many articles in local newspapers about the possible new cancer hospital. He responded sympathetically, clearly, and briefly to all inquiries. If there was any new measure to help patients he was intrigued, but if it was useless, he said so.

There are several dozen letters from concerned families he knew, asking his advice about a new miracle cure. His response to all such inquiries was that there was limited evidence, be careful, and that the writer should talk to his or her doctor. Occasionally he had the staff of the American Cancer Society seek data to clarify his answers. He gently dissuaded individuals who had heard of a vaccine that was actually of no value, or a peculiar diet that was reputed to cure cancer, or even the rampant enthusiasm about the notorious Krebiozin, a fruitless but one time popular "cancer cure." James, in 1954, and before the definitive trials of that soon controversial medication, had actually tried to obtain some for use by his own patients (115/1). He sent out inquiries about new or potential chemotherapeutic agents including triethylene thiophospharamide (120/1).

He made efforts himself to try new therapeutic approaches including trials of a new drug in 1957, Marsilid or isoproniazid, later primarily used as an anti-depressant (152/1). He initiated chemotherapy for his patients in 1960 with Cytoxan, cyclophosphamide. Convincing evidence of his commitment to research, if any were needed from this man who from the first written plans for a new hospital in 1963 listed more space for research (29,400 square feet) than for patient beds (117/11), is the enthusiasm with which he discussed plans with the radiation oncologist, Gahbauer, about "space age technology" (70/13). Topics included use of a cyclotron to create isotopes, boron neutron capture therapy, gamma knife technology, the linear accelerator, and use of radiation in the operating room.

The cyclotron story at OSU began early with a grant from Julius F. Stone in 1938 to build a cyclotron on the banks of the Olentangy River near where the Drake Performance and Event Center now stands (90/9). The Neoprobe, a small hand held detector of gamma signals, created a temporary flurry of enthusiastic support, as summarized in *Business Today*, June 21, 1993. It is still used, but very selectively. James, in his numerous lectures as the hospital began to take shape, spoke hopefully and often of "conformational radiology" which meant beams of destructive radiation selectively smashing into the tumor, not into the surrounding normal tissue (142).

The Connection with William G. Myers, M.D., Ph.D.

One of the special scientific friends of James was William G. Myers, M.D., Ph.D. Myers, who along with Ulrich K. Henschke, M.D., Ph.D., developed early radioisotopes at the time when, for a brief shining moment, OSU led the world in that technology. As isotopes were being proven useful for diagnosis, a second line of innovation, one valuable in therapy, was also launched by these two remarkable basic scientists.

Brachytherapy meant using radioactive materials placed in close (brachy) proximity to the cancer cells, and in the process of their research on isotopes the colleagues led the national development in brachytherapy. Employing gold threads made radioactive at the Oak Ridge National Laboratory in Tennessee, the innovators, along with Christoforidis and with James as the surgeon, placed snippets of the radioactive material directly in organs afflicted with cancer. One of the few areas in which this approach is still utilized is cancer of the prostate, but for a time James and the basic scientists led the field in use of radioactive gold filaments for insertion into neck tumors or tumors in the pelvis. Filaments were even employed as therapy for tumors of the breast. James published his observations and presented the results at several meetings (147/16). The group, in 1951, soon began to use radioactive cobalt rather than gold (147/10, 147/12).

The boron neutron capture story was not one in which James personally was heavily involved, but the OSU oncology program certainly was, and continues to be. Joseph Goodman, M.D., retired associate professor of neurosurgery, was of the opinion this technique, encouraged and funded by the federal government, had not been valuable and probably never would be. As summarized well by the still most active researcher in the field, Rolf Barth, M.D., there have never been optimal controlled studies using this technique to treat patients with brain tumors, the type of cancer that this experimental therapy was intended to ameliorate (Barth).

Dr. William G. Myers, leader in the development of radio-isotopes, examining gold seeds (Medical Heritage Center, William G. Myers, MD, PhD Collection)

Pyroscan, one of several efforts using thermography to track subtle temperature variations in the hope of identifying lesions, proved to be useless (125/1). While well aware of efforts to focus radiation, and of the need to identify metastatic lesions before and during surgery, James had to report that diagnostic techniques that relied on temperature gradients for diagnosis of breast cancer were of negligible value (117/52). On the other hand, this man, who in his presidential year with the ACS called for earlier, not just early, diagnosis of cancer, was among the first to diligently push mammography nationally and locally. James complained vigorously when the hours allowed for mammography testing were reduced at OSU in 1987 (123/13). Encouraging widespread use of that modality to diagnose, and his lifelong battle against the use of tobacco, represented his most consistent two efforts at cancer prevention.

James was curious about any potential environmental links to cancer, in hopes of discovering ways to prevent the disease. July 19, 1978, he carried on correspondence with Fred Zuspan, M.D., chair of the Obstetrics and Gynecology Department (126/25). The issue was whether estrogens might protect the patient; or, on the contrary, might turn out to enhance any tendency to develop cancer of the breast. James suggested: "It wouldn't be prudent to start off with a group of cancer patients and see if they were on estrogen, because we would have no idea of the estrogen use in the population....It might be significant, however, to determine the incidence of cancer among a group of women who have taken estrogen because this could be compared with the known incidence in the general population." Twenty five years later the answers were obtained and indeed there is now widespread awareness of potential complications from the use of estrogen. In 1987 James wrote Zuspan a personal note to thank him for "having been one person who always appreciated the cancer hospital plans."

Often the research planned or performed by James linked him with present or past professional colleagues. Because of his Duke ties as intern and in the military he undoubtedly had heard of the research of Joseph Markee, Ph.D., chair of the Anatomy Department at Duke. Markee had developed a technique of placing tissue into the anterior chamber of the eye to study growth, menstruation, etc. In May 1965, James requested funds from several potential sources to study the growth of cancer cells in the anterior chamber of the eye (117/16). This project never came to pass, not the grant nor publication of any such study. It seems probable that since he was receiving inquiries about that time regarding the potential value of vaccines, spoke often of eventual developments in that area and of chemotherapy, and did implant cancer cells as part of other studies, that he was looking for experimental models to test potential therapies for cancer.

James occupied many scientific committees for years, at least for as long as it furthered his goals. In addition to service for several national societies, he was chair of the local cancer committee for several decades, and a participant in committees that pushed cooperative research projects at OSU (122/1). Most of the research efforts at OSU that involved James were directly linked with therapy, and he was a strong proponent of medical therapy as well as of surgical approaches. A conspicuous example was the joining in 1978 of the oncology program of OSU with the Southwestern Oncology Group (SWOG) (125/29). This multi-institutional program, funded in large part by grants from federal scientific groups, organizes large protocol studies, combines data, and shares specimens and results. James, long before the hospital was a reality, argued that all patients should be on a program of therapy that would lead to information for others, and by that process doctors could investigate the most promising agents available. SWOG represents part of that continuing commitment at OSU, and every year new multi-institutional study groups are formed.

James' Published Scientific Papers

The over 100 scientific articles written by James are represented in the James collection, and many relate to the work mentioned above (147, 148). He had little time for basic research, but Frajola relates being sent by Doan down into the basement to find James who was trying out surgical approaches, using dogs as subjects. The extent of his research was reasonable for a busy surgeon, but almost all his reports were related to clinical issues. He certainly saw a great number of patients. When James discusses experience with thyroid cancer he speaks of 159 cases, of 308 patients with parotid tumors, and over 300 persons he saw with melanoma (147/29, 148/35). Even in a case report about a rare condition called mediastinal ganglioneuroma, published in 1941 with Curtis, who was his scientific mentor while James was in medical school, he culled 33 cases from the scattered literature to add to the one he had seen.

Occasionally a single unusual case or method attracted his attention, or a technique such as needle aspiration merited repeated explanations to his colleagues: "I feel better approaching a parotid tumor when I have had an aspiration biopsy" (111/31). As part of his interest in prognosis and in the survival of patients he frequently reviewed long-term results. He led many efforts to achieve complete cancer registries both in Columbus and nationally. From 1958 to 1964 James was editor of the Cancer Prognosis Manual sponsored by the American Cancer Society. Major interests during his career always included such surveillance records of the incidence of cancer, and the results of therapy (95/11).

His range of interest was wide, his reports were crisply written. He wrote of brothers with carotid body tumors (147/170), why failures may occur in cases with oral cancer (147/380), and why extensive surgery and dissection to halt cancer of the lip might be unwise (147/

31). He was particularly inclined to publish his observations if they could improve the effects of surgery. He wrote how to prevent accumulations of fluid after mastectomy (148/32), how to avoid trauma to the recurrent laryngeal nerve when operating nearby, how to patch the chest wall (147/4), and the best way to enhance movement of the arm after radical mastectomy (148/38). From the time of his thesis in medical school on iodine metabolism, his interest in the thyroid gland and cancers of the neck never waned (149/5). This was appropriately so in view of his mentors at Memorial, and also because the founding of the Columbus Cancer Clinic was really spurred by the thyroid disease that was so common at the time. Additionally, James published articles about diagnostic approaches in the rest of the body, including by mammography, and in 1952 he wrote of hormonal therapy to suppress cancer (147/13).

Professional Conflicts Stemming from his Research

There were of course disagreements to face. How could that not be in his vigorous world? Dr. George Crile, Jr., son of the legendary founder of the Cleveland Clinic, challenged James over the issue of radical breast surgery. In 1976 James invited Crile to Columbus, and later thanked him for his talk and for giving up his vacation time to visit (108/41). James, trained in the Halstead wide resection approach, fearless enough to perform even hemi-pelvectomy or the demanding "commando" neck surgery, considered removal of extensive tissue from around the tumor as offering the best chance of a complete cure from breast cancer. Crile, proponent of more limited surgical approaches, bridled in 1978 at James' written use of the word "lumpectomy" to describe what was being promoted at the Cleveland Clinic. James apologized for his verbal assault on local when compared to radical surgery on the breast, and the two eventually became mutually respectful leaders (107/36). James urged a test of the alternative methods of surgery in a direct comparison study. In fact that word, "lumpectomy," considered very offensive by Crile at the time (148/24), became commonly used, Crile's more conservative surgery was eventually the rule, and multiple cooperative studies became standard to define accepted surgical practices.

The most controversial single surgical investigation involving James was work performed during the 1950s in conjunction with Chester C. Southam, M.D., of Sloan–Kettering Research Institute, and later of Jefferson Medical College. Several dozen prisoners were enrolled, after approval by their local warden and after many prisoners in the local penitentiary had volunteered. In fact it was common to use prisoners at the time, and many volunteered eagerly; perhaps idealistically, perhaps to gain an edge for favors or consideration toward parole, perhaps simply to avoid boredom. As of 1982 medical experiments on prisoners were banned in Ohio, regardless of whether or not they volunteered. An article in *The Columbus Dispatch* on August 26, 1990, reports 169 prisoners were injected between 1956 and 1961, some with a second injection. James recalled: "the live cancers injected did develop cancers in each arm, tumors the size of walnuts" (JC 150). The tumor was excised and a second injection of cancer cells seemed to reveal less growth, presumably reflecting development of resistance. James wrote: "My role in that project was to surgically excise the tumors on the arms of the inmates which occurred following the inoculation of the cancer cells. [...] The original intent of the experiment was to see if a person who did not have cancer would kill cancer. We found he would" (115/1).

There was a prevailing concept at the time that failure of resistance of the body to cancer cells is what ultimately led to metastasis. Failure of resistance was considered the major factor that destroyed a patient, and the malignant cells themselves were not totally responsible for the uninhibited growth of cancer. This was at a time when investigators like James were well aware of the amazing protection from some infectious diseases conferred by vaccination, and immunology was a relatively new science.

A major problem in the cancer transplant work considered in our time, and James does deserve to be judged by his time, not by ours, is the use of prisoners for research projects. Most institutional review boards (IRBs), and none existed when this work was done, would now reject any research planned for prisoners. The incarcerated may not be able to give permission freely, and there may be powerful covert inducements to participate. The largest failure in the study, related to the patient group, was that prisoners were not followed adequately. Follow-up using their prison numbers proved insufficient to track the prior subjects (150/2).

James was not considered a major researcher by those in the walls of University Hospital, but how would James judge his own efforts at research, and what would be his message about research to his successors? He talked often of what he hoped would be the "half-life" of the ACS, convinced science was already a long way up the hill to cure cancer. He would probably offer his usual statement that in 1921 when the Free Clinic began, one in seven patients could be saved, that when he graduated from high school one in five was saved, and as he stepped down from his career one in three, or even one in two, was being cured. He was probably quietly proud of his own work, and by nature would have not have boasted of it. He often expressed a desire to see research progress on cancer, with results so useful that the James Cancer Hospital would be used for something other than cancer. To make that happy day come James told us to: continue what works, including developing more chemotherapy; encourage genetic studies; and, to look toward immunology and ways to enhance resistance (140/1).

"There is nothing more noble than to relieve human suffering."

Arthur G. James, M.D.

Chapter 12
Surgeon: This was first, last, and always, what James was

James' research, his basic livelihood, his motivation to be a doctor, all relate to the fact that he was a surgeon, and a fine one at that. Many of his friendships began through professional contacts, of course, but more than most surgeons he also maintained relationships with many grateful patients. He was well known, as noted above, for appearing at the hospital early in the morning, and in much of his career worked every day, even if only part of Saturday and Sunday. He liked Buckeye football, after all.

James regularly used the University operating rooms, of course, but for years did not limit himself to just one hospital. Most Columbus surgeons operated in several hospitals at the time, sometimes using as many as four different operating theatres in one month. Surgeons followed the patients, offered alternatives to them and responded to consultations from varied places. The surgeons were, after all, being supported primarily by private practice. Fostering personal and professional relationships in the community was crucial to assure referrals, and referrals were crucial for survival.

The schedule books maintained by Norma list names, the persons to contact, and the time for admission, since in earlier days most patients spent a day or more in the hospital before surgery. Finally, one sees what surgery was done, but the schedule book includes many other appointments. Even before the 1970s, James was committed at least once a week to give talks, often out of town, and there were scheduled times for teaching students, administrative meetings, etc. One can pick any week, however, and be sure he was busy, that he faced multiple challenges, and that he had to husband his time with care – there was always too little of it.

This is a typical week, January 28 to February 2, 1957, after James had been established for almost a decade in Columbus:

> 28th: Nevus removal, and breast surgery for cancer, at Mt. Carmel Hospital (on other occasions he operated at St. Anthony's or RMH)
>
> 29th: Thyroid removal, assist with appendectomy
>
> 30th: Breast excision, cancer of the palate
>
> 31st: Breast excision, radical neck surgery, thyroid surgery
>
> 1st: Breast cancer surgery, thyroid surgery

In 1961 he was performing surgical implantation of radioactive "seeds." Already in the late 1940s, and then into the 1970s, he was performing the "commando" procedure with its major dissection for cancer of the jaw or of the face (147/48). That composite surgical approach to oral facial cancer included resection of the tumor, dissection of the cervical lymph nodes, and even removal of the mandible, if necessary. He also did an occasional "hemipelvectomy," extensive removal of part of the lower body in an attempt to arrest cancer, and the report of five cases with this approach was published in 1962. During the busy 1960s, for over ten years Bonta was the very active partner in what was the major surgical cancer program in central Ohio.

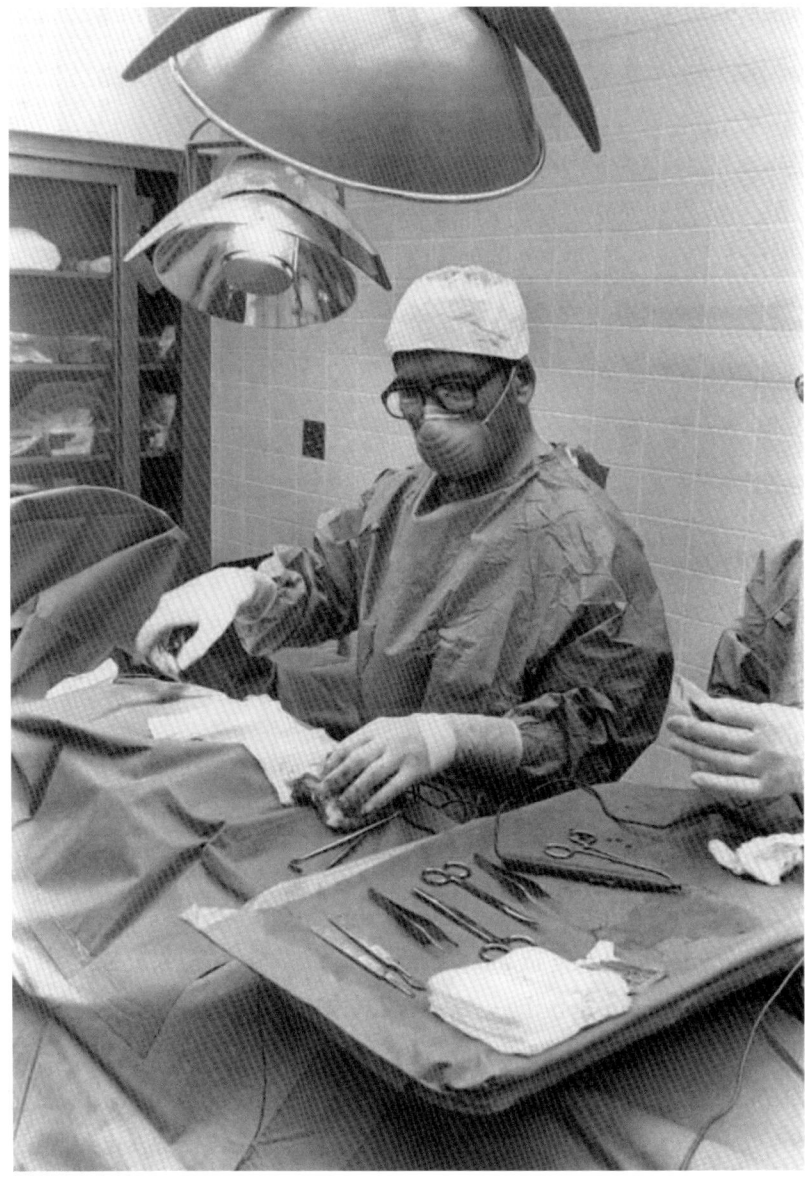

James operating (Medical Heritage Center, Arthur G. James, MD Collection)

director of the James Cancer Hospital, and a man who himself had served in the operating room with James, commented on James' courtesy, and on his respect for nurses. For example, in 1981 James was urging the opening of more nursing schools, and bemoaning the recent closure of the diploma schools in central Ohio (149/13). Smith also recalled an unanticipated cuff on the ear from a different professor, a blow that sat him down on the floor. He also recalled a fist fight by two other prominent surgeons in the dressing room, an unthinkable event in the presence of the dignified James.

James with Mrs. Charlotte Immke, Dr. David Schuller and Director Dennis Smith (Courtesy of Charlotte Immke)

The best teaching by surgeons, the teaching with the greatest impact in the future, is the mentoring a surgeon does with a junior colleague in the operating room. T. C. Mattison, M.D. wrote James on July 13, 1972: "I only felt finished in head and neck surgery after the experience with you. It is a pity that the rest of the Professional Staff at Ohio State cannot get this clear, that general surgery is at best only general and needs specific attention to details such as head and neck. I think that the university residents would be better if Zollinger realized it. I will be grateful to you for the rest of my life for the education you gave" (117/21). Dozens of former residents or interns solicited a letter of reference from James as they moved to a new position. They probably did so because he was well known, but we suspect also because they trusted him and were positive he would get the letter of reference written.

Unfortunately there is no way to accurately assess, to judge, a surgeon from the past. Comparative studies are difficult now and impossible in retrospect. Perhaps the proof of the pudding is in the eating. His patients loved him, his nurse was loyal for decades, and the multidisciplinary approach James absorbed at Memorial and conveyed to Columbus has changed the prognosis of cancer in the community. But we also note his work on behalf of individual patients everywhere. The devotion of grateful relatives, his surgical effort on behalf of thousands of sufferers, plus his willingness to get up on any platform to educate, encourage, and goad the public surely adds to the balance. And the balance for this surgeon is tilted positively.

"With a farsighted governor, a legislature concerned about the health of its constituency and an intelligent voting public, hopefully all the necessary ingredients are finally present that will result in Columbus obtaining the finest cancer hospital in the country."

Arthur G. James, M.D.

Chapter 13
Friends: the Dreamer had many helpful ones

Influential Friends and Patients

Even before reviewing a few of the hundreds of friends who joined James in his dream of better care for those afflicted with cancer in central Ohio, we should mention his style in counseling people he worked with on a daily basis. In interviews for this book members of the staff related their personal gratitude for advice or surgical help. One has to assume there were letters of reference he chose not to write, but the files contain over a hundred letters on behalf of various residents, interns, or prospective new medical students. His letters are always concise, often only a short paragraph, yet in addition to writing enough that it is clear he personally knew the applicant, there was specific confirmation of the applicant's skill and potential value to the next program. Frequently he mentioned the punctuality of the applicant, always an important consideration for James. There are several gentle letters to individuals who failed to get into OSU medical or dental schools, with James always suggesting continued effort, study, and a long range view of life. He maintained ties by responding to people in person and with letters, helping individuals as their physician and friend, and, it would seem, sometimes by just listening and being potentially available in time of need. It is not seemly to relate all the later financial contributors who for themselves, or for their family, had sought James for surgery, but a remarkably large number of the financial contributors to the programs he cared about had reason to be personally grateful for his efforts – as even now many people still contribute to The James Cancer Hospital because of a personal experience with cancer.

He clearly "stroked" his friends, good relationships do not survive by chance, and he welcomed a chance to praise or reward his associates. He recommended several colleagues for awards, including both Drs. Zollinger and Sid Nelson for distinguished teaching awards. He nominated Ed Moulton as chancellor to the Board of Regents. He recommended Mrs. Ellen Hardymon for a YWCA award in 1995, Vincent for an Alumni Achievement Award in 1982 (114/17), and Bonta for a recognition by the ACS in 1970 (109/19). In November 1973, James proposed Bonta for promotion to Clinical Associate Professor of Surgery. James was also quick to write thank you letters, and noted not just the deaths of acquaintances and the loss of his patients to cancer, but even wrote a kind note to the new beauty queen of St. Clairsville.

As hospital planning progressed, and particularly after the hospital became a reality, there appeared a steady stream of volunteer groups, civic organizations, high school classes, and others that were welcomed. All received entertainment and education while at OSU, particularly if such contact was likely to benefit the program. James invariably offered to escort them around the hospital, and did so whenever he was in town. He may have particularly enjoyed welcoming Queen Silvia of Sweden, who came on May 23, 1995, the visit of Mrs. Papanicolaou, and the large British contingent that came to study the hospital (109/25). He and the staff enthusiastically greeted Marilyn, the gracious wife of Vice President Dan Quayle (119/34). She had survived cancer herself, and came to help celebrate the opening of the cancer hospital. Such visits evolved into "Survivors Day" after a few years, a very large annual event with thousands present. James was probably responsible for the two visits by Dr. Judah Folkman, famous Harvard scientist whose father and aunt had assisted James with the Columbus Cancer Clinic. Folkman, who as student at OSU had worked with Doan, was the Landacre speaker for the student research group in 1987, and returned as the Herbert Bloch Memorial Lecturer in 1996 (117/50). James had once wished to attract him full time to OSU. At several events late in his life, and remembering his remarkable professional associates at OSU, James praised the deceased Drs. Doan, Henschke, Myers, Wilson, Wiseman and Zollinger (117/7). All had once joined him in the study and therapy of cancer patients.

There was ample opportunity to meet former interns or fellows from Memorial, Chicago, or Duke during the travels of James on behalf of the ACS, and even a chance in the West and in Alaska to fish with old friends, which he recalled later with delight. He did state, however, that the most fun of all was to fish with his sons in the pond at the farm in Delaware County, Ohio. This facility was used to solidify relationships. He and Millie often invited groups of friends and fellow cancer workers out to the farm, and with her in charge the events were invariably pleasant and the food delicious. Art and Millie were attentive hosts; and several dozen people seemed to consider themselves special friends of the couple. The examples mentioned are perhaps common for the friendships of any very successful surgeon, national figure, and academician who is genial and who marries a woman like Mildred Cameron. And there may have been none better as hostess and helpmate than his Millie.

Visit to the cancer hospital by Queen Silvia of Sweden (Medical Heritage Center, Arthur G. James, MD Collection)

Richard J. Solove

But one can argue that it was his sustained contacts with several dozen powerful, philanthropic, public-spirited, and influential individuals, his oh-so-successful local friends, which really turned the dream of a hospital into bricks and mortar. A good place to start is with Richard J. Solove, pharmacist, real estate developer, collector of rare automobiles, and philanthropist. The framework of his story is mirrored in the experience of others, and it was James as surgeon who made the first impact. Solove says that in 1953 when his father, an immigrant from Russia, twisted his neck a lump could be seen. The family doctor sent them to James' office on Neil Avenue, one with the calming aquarium that Solove still remembered four decades later. Within a few days James had removed the thyroid malignancy and begun thyroid replacement, leading to a lifetime friendship of Solove and James.

James with Mr. Richard Solove, leading developer, philanthropist and friend (Medical Heritage Center, Arthur G. James, MD Collection)

Solove and Millie (Courtesy of Norma Flesher, RN)

Perhaps the fact that the patient was an immigrant, and that both sons and fathers had worked hard to succeed, helped the men to understand one another. Solove found James "always positive, without vacillation about the need for the hospital, soft spoken, and quietly persistent." Solove remembered the meeting of the Columbus 16 at the Columbus Club on the night when the hospital really took shape in everyone's mind. When the project initially seemed blocked by Gordon Labuhn, Director of the Mid Ohio Hospital Planning Federation, over the issue of certificate of need, Governor Rhodes and Vern Riffe, Jr., encouraged by their mutual friend John W. Wolfe, managed simply to dissolve the board designed to issue such certificates. Another barrier was eliminated, and the dream remained alive.

Solove was one of many who contributed large amounts of money and time to make the hospital a reality. In 1999 the hospital name was changed to acknowledge his generous contributions, including one of $20 million, which at the time was said to be the third largest the University had ever received. The official name is now "The Arthur G. James Cancer Hospital and Richard J. Solove Research Institute." Solove modestly calls it, as do most others, simply "The James."

R. David Thomas

R. David Thomas was another, and equally interesting, major contributor. He began his financial contributions in 1975 (147). His first contributions were to the Columbus Cancer Clinic, and consisted of stock to be utilized when a hospital was finally built. Thomas is the now legendary founder of Wendy's Old Fashioned Hamburgers, an international fast food chain, named for his daughter, that began in 1969. This open hearted philanthropist gave generous gifts to Duke as well as to OSU. Adopted as an infant he never knew his biological parents. He established the Dave Thomas Foundation for Adoption

R. David Thomas, Founder of Wendy's with James (Medical Heritage Center, Arthur G. James, MD Collection)

to encourage the adoption process everywhere. He never had a chance to finish high school, although later in life he did obtain a GED, but he well deserved his reputation as an intelligent, caring, and diligent businessman. His genial good humor and "down home" style allowed him to succeed in hundreds of advertisements for his hamburger chain, one that within only a few decades became one of the most popular fast food programs in history. Thomas was one of several who admired James because of personal experience with him as physician and man, and perhaps there was comfort in similarly humble backgrounds.

Leonard J. Immke

Leonard J. Immke, Len to all, and a very successful owner of automobile dealerships in Columbus, was a proud member of the Board of Trustees of OSU. He also was a man with less than an extensive education, and he was involved with the Wendy's story from its inception. The relationship reportedly began when Thomas and

Charlotte and Len Immke, longtime supporters of James, the hospital and OSU (Courtesy of Charlotte Immke)

Immke left the Athletic Club together, hungry, and wished a hamburger shop was nearby. Immke said he would supply space across from his dealership at 5th Ave and Broad Street if Thomas could run the shop. S. Robert Davis, real estate developer and another early stockholder in the new Wendy's enterprise, soon joined the group beginning to support the efforts of James. Another example of the multiple linkages at the time, Mrs. Charlotte Immke says they first met Dr. and Mrs. James because "Manuel and Madeline Tzagournis invited us out to dinner with the Jameses."

James and S. Robert Davis, an early stockholder in Wendy's (Medical Heritage Center, Arthur G. James, MD Collection)

Governor Rhodes, a man crucial for the dream of a hospital, encouraged both Wendy's and Dave Thomas, and was often present among the group of responsive friends around Thomas and Immke. Several other members of the circle around Thomas and Immke were included in the group that visited the Anderson and Memorial Cancer Hospitals. The names of those travelers who flew off to enthusiastically explore possibilities for the hospital are listed elsewhere. Most were local corporate and financial titans, and all counted James among their friends. Importantly for this story, all were men others would follow, even in philanthropy.

James and Governor James Rhodes, staunch supporter of James and of OSU, October 1990 (Medical Heritage Center, Arthur G. James, MD Collection)

James the Fundraiser

James had a remarkable ability to ask such friends, in fact often his close and well heeled friends, for money for research and for the care of those with cancer. James himself eventually became a member of the Board of Directors for Development at OSU (114/14), by then having had adequate experience with fundraising for the United Way, for the Columbus Cancer Clinic, and in 1984 for the Society of Surgical Oncology (117/43). He made several detailed lists of prospective donors for the cancer hospital, and contacted many of them directly.

He was not always initially successful in his efforts to get money for the battle against cancer. Several letters were sent to the Walton family, founders of Wal-Mart (114/15), and clearly many were similarly contacted who have not yet contributed significantly, but he tried again and again. Sometimes success was unexpected, and if so was quickly urged along by James. Walter J. Frajola, biochemist and dear friend of Doan, recounts the story of an accountant whose client was unhappy that he never received thanks for his largess to the OSU Stone Laboratories at Lake Erie. James immediately offered to escort the accountant, the potential donor, and their wives, around the framework going up for the hospital. As he did so he told them what would be located where, and why, and how it mattered. The donor added more money, and more importantly, shifted his contribution to the cancer hospital.

Once James said there had been over 250 meetings during the overall planning stage for the hospital, and he clearly had even more contacts for fundraising. It seems likely that he also conducted almost as many tours to educate the public, and certainly he made sure any gift, even any potential gift, was acknowledged. The same man who had once been a boy carefully tending his parents' grocery store during the depression was meticulous about money. When Ivan Gilbert, who knew James during his entire career, was asked how a physician could be so effective in raising money, he replied: "He was always asking for a cause he believed in, not ever for himself."

"The secret of success is perseverance… Learn early not to leave a worthwhile thing undone."

Arthur G. James, M.D.

Chapter 14
Investor: the boy who once worked in a grocery store became a man who invested

There are lessons to be learned from the approach of James to investments, and his style was similar to his approach to any issue. Effort, forethought, reliance on friends, and common sense combined with persistence were in evidence once again. He succeeded in his investments, and his family insisted he made more money from wise investments than from surgery. He was never profligate, always punctual in paying his bills, and equally scrupulous about not being overcharged. This child of the Great Depression, although often generous, remained aware of the value of money always.

His family lived modestly in their nice but not palatial home at 1911 Waltham Road in Upper Arlington, and he probably helped his father in the purchase of a small grocery after his parents moved to Columbus. Later Dr. and Mrs. James lived in a convenient double condominium in Upper Arlington. But his major investments were not in a regal private home.

James retained frugal and careful personal habits, and when he left the military after 44 months of active duty service he probably carried financial assets along with his return baggage. He had a young family to support but also wanted more education in cancer research and in the care of patients. His savings, plus possibly with help from the G.I. Bill, facilitated living in New York while he completed the fellowship at Memorial.

James purchased his first office building early in his practice, taking out a loan of $49,000 on October 27, 1952 (125/22). The initial mortgage deed for the office lists both Mildred James and Arthur, but also Millie's brother, Robert V. Cameron, so there may have been family help in this purchase, one of the earliest of many wise investments. He successfully appealed to Columbus city officials on March 17, 1953, to have the office at Neil re-zoned commercially from C-1 to E-1 (125/1). The monthly payment for the loan was $514, probably met by the rental from four one room efficiency apartments on the second floor, plus a similar group on the third floor. When he borrowed another $25,000 in September 1954, to remodel a section of the office to accommodate radiological equipment, he said the rentals produced approximately $500 per month. He argued for a larger settlement when the University threatened to take it by eminent domain. He was not only losing his property, which he had expected to happen because of the growth of OSU, he was also to lose a source of income from the rented efficiency apartments.

The successor to the office at Neil Avenue was the one at Olentangy River Road, and as with his first building he renovated and successfully rented sections of it. The initial renters continued there for years. As for how James was a landlord, the highly respected cardiologist, Raymond Barker, M.D., wrote on March 17, 2008: "It has been a pleasure to look back on the practice of medicine. Arthur James played an important part in that period. The first thing I remember was on a Christmas Eve, Art and his sons came to my home to deliver

Neil Avenue office building coming down (Medical Heritage Center, Arthur G. James, MD Collection)

a gift. When White Cross moved to RMH he gave me the opportunity to move into the office building he was establishing near RMH. He made sure every thing was first class. If there was any problem I would talk to him or Norma and it would be promptly resolved. I remained in that office until I retired." James continued aware of the needs of people on his property and there are several nice letters from the men who lived or worked on the varied farms he owned at one time or another, including a letter thanking James for his effort at compensation after a fire destroyed one of the barns.

There are several letters in the James Collection from a real estate developer in the Delaware area who regularly contacted James with suggestions for potential purchases of land. James and his children frequently drove around the countryside looking for likely prospects for investment. His son David remembered his dad had always wanted a farm for the boys to enjoy, but also sought a farm because throughout all his own boyhood he had wanted a pony. There was no way Abramo or Rosa could divert money from food, education, or clothes to buy a horse, but James made sure his own children got the experience of being on horseback. So he purchased several farms in Ohio.

A farm of 232 acres in Harrison Township near Pataskala was purchased in 1968. He once purchased a 124.56 acre farm in Berlin Township. There was also a farm near Delaware, and that, according to Norma, was bought with awareness, perhaps anticipation, that the Alum Creek Reservoir would eventually take part of that property from him, but would surely offer adequate compensation. The property was located on S. Old State Road at Peachblow Road in Delaware County. In July and August of 1961 he contacted public officials for details about a proposed Alum Creek Dam, and obtained a map from the U. S. Army Corps of Engineers (124/26). Many of the later parties for friends and donors were at another patch of land located at 1010 Africa Road, a place he called ArtMil Acres. He made sure there was a pond for fishing on that property.

Adjacent to the office on Olentangy River Road there was vacant property which was developed into a hotel that remains on that site. He owned several acres along Bethel Road, and in 1969 a prominent local man wanted to buy that parcel, but James said no thanks. The land is about where a "surgi-center" is currently located, across the street from a major shopping center. He owned a swath of land along Africa Road near the current Polaris. Much of his property was eventually developed in varied ways, and at the time of his death his sons report that he owned about a thousand or more acres of land in Franklin, Delaware and Licking counties (39).

His friendships, sincere and lasting ones, with the major developers in town undoubtedly expedited his acquisitions. James became a Wendy's franchise owner in Massachusetts and in Rhode Island for a short time due to his association with Dave Thomas and with Mike Scanlon, his stock broker, who commented they were lucky to get out of it without more loss than they had. James once purchased land in Connecticut in hopes of owning a Wendy's franchise there (121/11).

James wrote more than once that his hobby was fishing, whether in his farm pond of one acre in Delaware County, on Thomas' yacht in Florida, in Wyoming with his older brother Felix, or in Alaska as the guest of fellow American Cancer Society volunteers and physicians. Thomas also enjoyed fishing, at least fishing with James, and there have been few entrepreneurs in Columbus who were more pleasant or more loyal to his friends than Thomas. Dr. and Mrs. James particularly relished fishing in the Florida Keys, enough so that they purchased a condominium at MM 75 in Lower Metacumbe, just south of Islamorada. They enjoyed entertaining family and friends there in the early 1970s. Mounted fish on the walls, innumerable photographs that Millie made, and stacks of "thank you" cards testify to that happy time.

The only good reason to discuss the possessions of James is to use his style in investments to highlight his basic characteristics. He watched for opportunities, was never fixed on holding onto a piece of property, and tended to turn one investment into two. As with his military time he was not prone to brag of success nor did he complain of failure, and while not secretive he was circumspect in his choice of possessions and wise in his plans for development. He turned to his friends, as they did to him. His friends, including developer Jack Havens, were often helpful with suggestions. As at work, James always

Good times in Key West, Art in striped shirt, Millie in glasses (Medical Heritage Center, Arthur G. James, MD Collection)

(Medical Heritage Center, Arthur G. James, MD Collection)

wore a suit and tie when he visited the farms, but had the ability to talk easily to people working in the field. He could even be shrewd. His son David remembered a negotiation when a man who wished to buy property from James handed over a piece of paper on which he had written the price he would pay. James studied the paper, handed it back, and said gently "you are close," so the purchaser added more. The deal was settled. When David later asked his father what he had expected, James said he had actually anticipated a much lower offer than the first one.

He grew up in the Depression and hated to waste money. There are several letters in the files pointing out to a hotel or to traffic authorities that he actually owed one or two dollars less than he had been charged. There are several letters inquiring about the stability of a company he had become interested in. But there are many more letters thanking someone for an item he had purchased by mail, one that he considered was just what he wanted.

What were the major traits of his investment style? For one thing all those important friendships were clearly a feature, Scanlon and Havens remain loyal to his memory today. Another was James' curiosity. If he was driving around town and thought an area was likely to grow, he watched it for opportunities nearby. He was kind and professional with any renters, quick to pay his own debts, and content to keep his personal matters totally out of the limelight. Except, of course, for those matters related to the hospital that became his passion, and for that he sought all the publicity possible.

"I agreed to accept this award so I could get out word about the hospital."

Arthur G. James, M.D.

Chapter 15
Accolades: the Dreamer accepts praise, and then uses it to push for his dream

Recognitions

We have already mentioned some of the many plaudits James received; there is little wisdom in reviewing them all. No one can be sure which award pleased him the most, or which did the most to push his cause forward. The latter purpose, to create the cancer hospital, was always in his mind. Several times in accepting a request to come for an award he stated the real reason he was pleased to be honored was to direct attention to the cancer hospital. *The Columbus Dispatch* was a help, and could always be depended on to report the events that acknowledged James. That newspaper, its owners, and its editors were among the most faithful supporters of James and of his frequently discussed cancer hospital. Even the other current newspaper of the time, *The Columbus Citizen Journal*, cited him as one of the top ten men in Columbus in 1973 (JC 150).

Less visible than events in Columbus, but surely equally pleasant, was being asked to give the honorary address to surviving high school classmates 50 years after graduation. From his medical school he received the Alumni Achievement Award in September 1977. And it must have been a delight to receive an "exemplary teaching award" from his Department of Surgery. This was followed two years later by the second ever Resident's Award for Excellence in Teaching, just after his particularly busy year of 1977. The students in the medical school had already chosen him, in 1963, for honorary membership in their national honor society, Alpha Omega Alpha, a group that selects honor students and a few faculty. He was the recipient of the Lucy Wortham James Clinical Research Award over two decades later, further confirming him as a serious academician (117/10).

On essentially every such honorific occasion James offered comments, usually from note cards, and occasionally he referred to a typed sheet prepared for him by Norma from the cards. The themes of the talks were always similar: Thank you for this honor, we have come a long way in cancer therapy, we will go further, cancer will be cured, and we need a cancer hospital in Columbus. One of the few phenomena that suggested a modicum of hypocrisy in James was his often stated surprise at receiving one or another award.

After serving on eleven of its committees, becoming a member of the Board of Directors of the American Cancer Society, and since he had served in every official position, it is no surprise that the Society in 1981 awarded James an honorary Life Membership, and then a special gold medal for his lifetime of service.

Two other special awards can not be ignored. Both were a reminder to all of James' humble beginnings, and of his unassuming manner despite the bright light of success. These were the Horatio Alger Award, with membership into the Horatio Alger Association of Distinguished Americans, and then being the honoree of the St. John the Baptist Church Italian Festival.

Horatio Alger, Jr. and the Association that Bears his Name

Horatio Alger, Jr. (1832-1899), wrote more than 125 rags-to-riches novels such as Ragged Dick and Tattered Tom (60/1-8). In his time, the Victorian era, Alger was second only to Mark Twain in popularity. Alger was an avowed salesman for the American dream, and most of his tales were about a lad who started from scratch and who despite great odds reached the top. The author himself was sickly and suffered from asthma as a child, but was able to enter Harvard at age 16 and led a vigorous, varied, and useful life. He was for a time a newspaperman and correspondent, a scholar and friend of poets, a minister, and then he achieved success with his pen. His stories were stereotyped, tales of success despite all odds. In his personal life he tried hard to retrieve boys who were just drifting, particularly homeless newsboys. Our modern age of cynicism has noted most of the heroes in the novels depended on a wealthy patron for help, and even in his own time this novelist and part time minister had the purity of his motives questioned. He did expend much of his personal income to help indigent youths, however, and housed some of the lost boys himself. His name has become synonymous for a rise to fortune through hard work and perseverance.

In keeping with the spirit of the American dream, and in a desire to reward outstanding individuals who embody that dream despite modest beginnings, the Horatio Alger Association of Distinguished Americans was founded in 1947. The Creed of the group, "to modern ears sounding like the product of another and perhaps more innocent age," was prepared by Norman Vincent Peale (1898-1993), the minister who expounded the "Power of Positive Thinking." The Creed emphasized the importance of honesty, morality, integrity, individual initiative, creative enterprise, hard work, and a determination to give adherence to the ideals of service to one's fellow man.

Art and Millie with Ruth and Dean Jeffers at the occasion of the Horatio Alger Award (Courtesy of James Family)

In 1987 the Horatio Alger Association honored the coal miner's son from Southeastern Ohio. Letters nominating James for this award were sent by Governor James A. Rhodes, Congressman Chalmers Wylie, Charles Lazarus, chair of Lazarus Company, members of national and state cancer communities, Congressman Wayne Hays, Jack Havens, chair of Banc One Corporation and of the Board of Trustees of OSU, R. David Thomas, founder of Wendy's, Dean Jeffers, chair of Nationwide Insurance, and John P. McConnell, chair of Worthington Industries. The last three were the only people from Columbus that had ever been similarly honored. James was one of ten distinguished Americans who were selected that year for the award, and he invited family and friends to Chicago for the ceremony to see him with the young students who were being honored with scholarships. In later years James contributed to those youth scholarships, giving $1,000 in 1990 (120/8).

Governor Rhodes's letter stated: "He was born amidst the humblest circumstances and through hard work, diligence, dedication, and commitment to his fellow men, has risen to a place of great prominence in the world medical community. I have known this fine man for more than 35 years. As Mayor of Columbus and later as Governor of Ohio, I watched him as he relentlessly pursued his dream – the establishment of a full-fledged cancer hospital at the OSU Hospitals, the only such hospital between New York City and the State of Texas.

There is no way to capture in words the dedication he has to the healing of people. You have to know him and observe him as he quietly works towards that noblest of goals. During the period he served so ably as President of the ACS, great strides were made in cancer research and treatment.

James is not only an esteemed, learned physician, he is truly one of the world's great humanitarians."

The Italian Festival and the Christopher Columbus Award

There may be less national fame for the Italian Festival of Columbus than for the Horatio Alger Award banquet, but the meeting in Columbus was probably a lot more fun. After all, it fit with James' heritage and included many friends. The Italian Festival has met at more than one place, but usually near St. John the Baptist Catholic Church. The spaghetti meal at the church would have been delicious; certainly visitors to the festival mention mouthwatering aromas, friendly people, and music in the air. At the 1995 Italian Festival, James was recognized by the Italian community as the honoree, a portrait was painted, and he was inducted into the Italian Cultural Center Hall of Fame. He was also recognized by other Italian organizations at various times, such as the Columbus Piave Club, and the Christopher Columbus Education Foundation who presented James with its Lifetime Achievement Award. This award was linked to an annual scholarship in his honor. Also in 1995, James received the prestigious Governor's Award, from then Ohio Governor George Voinovich.

He had already received an Outstanding Achievement Award from the Realtors Association in 1987, and then in 1991 the OSU Alumni Medalist Award. The Ohio Hospital Association Award honored him in 1992 for meritorious service, and also that year he was honored with the Lung Association award entitled "The Columbus Greats We Love." In 1993 he received the Franklinton Award for outstanding contributions to the community, and then the Columbus Foundation Award for community service in 1994. There were even posthumous awards. His visage and accomplishments appear in bronze outside the Upper Arlington City Hall. And then there was a last honor when Major Arthur James of the 65th Army Hospital was inducted into the Ohio Veterans Hall of Fame in 2006. At least with the Italian Festival award there was his beloved spaghetti, and he could be there to enjoy it.

James, surrounded by Millie, David, and Cameron, presented by Pat Rossetti with a portrait at the 1995 Hall of Fame induction at the Italian Festival (Courtesy of the Columbus Dispatch)

Plaque honoring James, placed on the wall at Upper Arlington Municipal Center (Courtesy of George Paulson, MD)

"When you believe in something you shouldn't be discouraged by a delay. You have to show perseverance."

Arthur G. James, M.D.

Chapter 16
The Dream Becomes Concrete: steps toward the dream

How the Hospital Came to Be

When James returned from Memorial to Columbus in 1948 after World War II, he was keenly aware that there was no designated cancer hospital between New York and Texas. That fact was reflected in the consistent drumbeat in his letters and speeches during the next four decades. He personally did well, that is no surprise, as he established a surgical practice focused on cancer. Within only a few years he was recognized as the leading cancer surgeon in the area. Before he came, the extensive "commando" procedure had never previously been attempted in Columbus, but James did it. The young surgeon noted, however, that he was on the phone several times each week seeking counsel from his mentors at Memorial. He missed the input of other experts who were at a cancer center such as the one at Memorial, and he soon set out to build an equivalent program in Columbus.

In 1962, on its front page, the *Columbus Dispatch* presented the concept of a cancer hospital as a real possibility (JC 150). This tangible proof of the support of the powerful and public spirited publisher

John W. Wolfe was a most promising omen for the future. Typical for the man, he never withdrew his ardent support. Several original plans of the Columbus Cancer Clinic suggested placing the hospital in unused portions of Grant Hospital, in the Old White Cross building at Goodale Park, or in the Ben Franklin Tuberculosis Hospital. The Columbus Hospital Federation rejected any such Columbus Cancer Clinic plan (19).

After that rebuff, in 1963 James met with the visionary CEO of Riverside Methodist Hospital, Edgar Mansfield, and the two agreed to seek a hospital of 29,000 square feet to serve 100 patients. It was to be located adjacent to RMH (117/11). The letter of agreement on February 28, 1963, also planned an additional 29,400 square feet designated for research, with 30,000 square feet for service area and at a total cost of $3,035,800 (117/1). Probably because of lack of support by the Riverside medical staff this project never got past the planning stage.

In 1964 in letters exchanged with the assistant director of Memorial, James listed major reasons a cancer hospital was needed. In fact this list was almost exactly the same one he used for several decades: A) concentration of patients with one disease facilitates study; B) data can be accumulated for cooperative research studies in a centralized facility; C) a concentration of patients with cancer is better for training specialists in the discipline; D) a larger, and clearly concentrated, facility is more likely to obtain funding; E) local population will be more aware, more involved, and more likely to donate to a designated facility; and, F) for education, service, and care, centralization will be better (152/8).

Effort to garner community support led James, ostensibly speaking for the Columbus Cancer Clinic, once again formally to seek the approval of the Columbus Hospital Federation. Its Director,

Delbert L. Pugh, remained dubious and on July 13, 1964 suggested the Franklin County Academy of Medicine should be consulted. On July 21st Homer Anderson, M.D., president of the Academy, reported the negative decision of the Council of the Academy: "They could not support the proposal for a special cancer hospital in this area."

In the 1970s Governor James Rhodes, influenced by James and Wolfe of the *Columbus Dispatch,* began to talk of a state bond issue, one that would include commitment to build a cancer hospital. Rhodes was out of office from 1970 to 1974. In 1973, after Nixon and Congress had declared war on cancer, OSU established a Cancer Research Center. In 1974 planning for the hospital was still linked by James with the Columbus Cancer Clinic, but the projected cost of the hospital had risen to $25 million.

In 1975, while continuing to use the Columbus Cancer Clinic as his institutional base, James submitted an application to the Mid Ohio Health Planning Federation to construct a 200 bed free-standing cancer hospital at a cost of $30 million. Despite declining patient counts, and spiraling costs, OSU submitted its own competing letter of intent to build a 200 bed facility only four months after the application by James. Governor Rhodes, demonstrating as much resilience as James, was re-elected for an unprecedented third term after being out of office for four years. In 1975 voters turned down the re-elected Governor Rhodes's new capital improvement budget, funds which might have supported one, but certainly not both, of the two hospitals being proposed.

In 1977 the National Cancer Institute (NCI) designated OSU one of 18 initial Comprehensive Cancer Centers in the United States. By 1992 there were 28 such centers plus many more units devoted exclusively to cancer (95/2). James had been at the front during this wave of advances. He had testified before Congress on behalf of that legislation, but at first was not heavily involved with the local basic research center at OSU (114/10). Nevertheless, he and key members of the Columbus Cancer Clinic continued busily discussing the possibility of a free standing cancer hospital. By 1977 there were two "CCCs" in the Columbus area: (1) Comprehensive Cancer Center and (2) Columbus Cancer Clinic. Each was well aware, and largely supportive, of the other. It was necessary at times, certainly later, to clarify the administrative structure of the program at OSU, and as sometimes can happen the culture of the basic scientists and that of surgeons required more understanding than was automatic (126/12). The Director of the Center, David Yohn, PhD., M.P.H., was a respected basic scientist and administrator who clearly appreciated the efforts of James to help secure the program. In fact Yohn wrote James a gracious thank you letter on January 30, 1974.

Yohn, was, nevertheless, not completely at ease about the possible presence of two programs at OSU doing the same work, competing for the same funds, or run with less than clear control by the University (98/2). Director Yohn on September 10, 1975 wrote that he could not support a separate department of clinical oncology within the College of Medicine (14/39). A national survey team from the NCI soon commented forcefully, however, that the director of the Comprehensive Cancer Center lacked sufficient autonomy to achieve a first class program. The seemingly ever recurring issue of how much autonomy was ideal to secure funds and future development appeared again. A litany of the dozens of meetings to iron out the ideal relationship between the prospective cancer hospital and the existing Comprehensive Cancer Center would be more confusing than it would be wise. The different points of view of clinicians and basic scientists, the issue of who gets space and money, the varied styles of the participants are almost too complex to interpret accurately. In a letter

December 31, 1981, Yohn again expressed continued concern about the relationship between the Comprehensive Cancer Center at OSU and the cancer hospital, which by then was becoming more and more likely to appear (126/12). The final upshot, one James would have encouraged and did help bring to pass, is that the programs are fused as much as is possible, with cooperation now between seven interdisciplinary programs from 12 out of the 18 colleges on campus, and with over 250 individual investigators. There is also cooperative linkage with the Children's Hospitals in both Columbus and Cincinnati.

Even before 1974, James had defined his criteria for an ideal cancer hospital: A) Above all, there should be autonomy for the hospital. Even if the program was to result from a joint effort by the Columbus Cancer Clinic and OSU, the hospital should be responsible for its own fate. B) A full time staff, not occasional participating or visiting physicians, was needed. C) A research focus was mandatory along each step of the way, and almost all patients should be on a research protocol. D) A separate (federal) billing process should be sought to maintain integrity and to enhance collections (56/8). If these seem repetitive from before, they were repetitive, indeed were so for over three decades.

Nevertheless, not everyone agreed with the need for any specialty cancer hospital. Criticism or concern about the effect of the hospital on the community appeared, including comments on January 1984 from George Clouse, M.D. and comments in the local Academy *Bulletin* (114/1). Informal conversation at meetings, and efforts at closed door persuasion might have halted a more fragile, or a less determined, man. In 1974 in a letter to a colleague at his beloved Memorial, James had already reported he was being "greatly sniped at" (122/22). There was both support and unease about the proposed hospital throughout the medical community, of course, and finally the scrupulous, even demanding, editor of the *Bulletin of the Academy of Medicine of Franklin County*, Warren Smith, M.D. asked James to write an article entitled "Why Columbus should have a Cancer Hospital" (123/23). Smith added: "Ever since I have been in Columbus, it has been clear to me that you hold a rather unique position in the medical community; you are regarded as an outstanding authority in your field and, at the same time, are beloved by colleagues as well as patients. I have never heard a negative statement expressed about Art James, and I don't know any other medical luminary who is held in such esteem." That may have been true, but from multiple interviews it has been apparent that some of the physicians in Columbus who did respect him, and some of the faculty at the OSU Medical College who similarly respected him, were not at all enamored with the goals of Arthur G. James.

Ohio Cancer Hospital Foundation

In January 1976, James led the establishment of the Ohio Cancer Hospital Foundation with Articles of Incorporation (14/29, 92/2), and he was greatly encouraged in that effort on March 28, 1977 at a meeting in the Columbus Club by sixteen of Columbus's most successful business men. Most members of the original board of the Foundation remained active for over a decade (92/3). The planned hospital, the primary goal of the new Foundation, was to be a free-standing, not-for-profit and autonomous institution. It is of interest in view of that continued issue, that James even added a longhand note to the original draft: "including complete budgetary and program control of the hospital." The plan was for the trustees of the Foundation to include James as well as the Dean of the Medical School, plus three more from OSU and three from the Columbus Cancer Clinic. Furthermore, if there was no hospital by 1986 the

James in 1972 (Medical Heritage Center, Arthur G. James, MD Collection)

Foundation was to be dissolved. James was the Chief Medical Officer (117/17). On December 15, 1980, all assets of the Foundation were transferred to the Columbus Cancer Clinic, and those intended for the building were eventually used for that purpose. Contributions from many sources appeared during this time of steadily rising expectations. Dave Thomas gave almost 20,000 shares of Wendy's stock on October 4, 1977, and another 90,000 shares on January 27, 1983.

Herbert Cook, Jr., explained the significance of this group:
> Then James announced formation of the Ohio Cancer Foundation, a private, non-profit group whose sole purpose was to finance and build the long-awaited hospital. The announcement rated a banner headline in *The Columbus Dispatch*, and the foundation's initial board of trustees – many of whom had accompanied James to Houston six months earlier – looked like a Who's Who of the Columbus Power structure. In addition to Wolfe, Davis, Thomas, and Kessler, the board included Battelle President Sherwood Fawcett; developer and banker John F. Havens, Huntington Bancshares President Arthur Herrmann; Buick dealer and OSU trustee Len Immke; Nationwide Insurance Chief Executive Dean Jeffers; Lazarus Chairman Charles Y. Lazarus; Worthington Industries Chief Executive John McConnell; First Bank Group Chair John G. McCoy; realtor and developer James Petropoulos; and developer Richard Solove. It may have been the most powerful nonprofit board ever assembled in Columbus, and it was a testimony to the labors of Art James, a master at keeping his fences mended. (60/8, 92/2)

On February 25, 1976, after James had written to him of his new Foundation designed to lead to a cancer hospital, the Dean of the College of Medicine, Vice President Henry Cramblett wrote: "On behalf of The Ohio State University, I regret to inform you that I do not view favorably the organization of a corporation 'for the purpose of planning, financing, constructing, equipping, and operating a free standing not-for-profit hospital and related facilities for the complete care and management and treatment of patients suffering from cancer and allied diseases and for other related activities…'" (108/38).

The reasons given by Cramblett were: 1) There had been no demonstrable need for additional beds. 2) OSU would not transfer patients to such a facility. 3) University Hospital would need 200 beds of its own for cancer patients by 1980. 4) The people of Ohio would suffer because the OSU programs would be splintered by such a program. 5) The efforts to build a hospital would mean OSU would be soliciting funds for three competing programs. These were the College of Medicine and Development Fund, OSU Cancer Center, and the projected new Ohio Cancer Hospital Foundation.

OSU President Enarson, who worked closely with Cramblett, had a great deal on his plate at the time, including the effort to clarify rules for private practice at the medical center. There was probably concern that if the legislature was pushed to supply funds for a new hospital other capital programs might suffer. Cramblett was a leader among the key administrators who eventually did become very influential as planning for the hospital got underway. Cramblett was a pediatrician, microbiologist, founder of a department, and then served as Dean of the College of Medicine from 1973 to 1980. He was active in obtaining endowed chairs and very effective in working with senators and legislators at a time the funding for the cancer center was in doubt.

By October 6, 1976 it became obvious, obvious even to James, that OSU considered it necessary to refuse, resolutely, to be involved. So he proceeded again to try to do it alone, again as an arm of the Columbus Cancer Clinic. He continued to raise funds, link the movers and shakers of Columbus to the effort, and gave speech after speech in the community. At the same time he was the busiest surgeon in town in treating patients with cancer, and he carefully maintained contact with many of his loyal patients. They, his board at the Columbus Cancer Clinic, and Rhodes, in particular, had never given up. Solove and Havens give much credit to Publisher John W. Wolfe, who was in close contact with not only Republican Governor Rhodes, but also with Democrat Vern Riffe, Jr., the powerful Speaker of the House of the Ohio Legislature. Rhodes and Riffe took a firm leadership role in getting legislative support.

The story had many twists and turns and the best summary may be that of Cook in the *Columbus Monthly* of January 1980 (60/8): Cook's article begins by describing the "power" trip of James and his friends to the University of Texas M. D. Anderson Cancer Hospital (M.D. Anderson) in November 1976 (123/29). At the time Anderson, established in 1941, was one of only three major cancer hospitals in America, three after Roswell Park joined M.D. Anderson and Memorial as "free standing" national centers of research and therapy in 1971. The Director of M.D. Anderson, Lee Clark, M.D., was a personal friend of James. *Dispatch* Publisher John Wolfe supplied a plane to get the group to Houston. Paul Metzger, M.D., who made the trip as the Chief Medical Officer of Nationwide, and former president of the Franklin Academy of Medicine, remembered an impassioned presentation by Clark emphasizing the need for autonomy for the cancer hospital. After two days of instruction in oncology and tours of the facility at Anderson some members in the group were willing to write a check to support a similar hospital in Columbus.

Verne Riffe, prominent legislator and supporter of the hospital, statue located in the Riffe Building, Columbus (Courtesy of George Paulson, MD)

Mid Ohio Planning Federation

There was one dissenting voice, however, and it came loud and clear from Gordon M. Labuhn, the Executive Director of the Mid Ohio Hospital Planning Federation (MOHPF). An attempt to interpret MOHPF is not the purpose of this book, but that group represents an interesting local story. After World War II there was a flush of cooperation between hospitals in central Ohio, spurred on by $50 million in funds for construction, potential new bond issues, and the crushing need for more inpatient beds. The cooperation, not destined to remain forever, produced several groups, one of which was the Columbus Hospital Federation. This in turn led to what was called the Hospital Commission, lineal predecessor of the current Franklin County Hospital Commission. The current Commission is a group that approves plans for borrowing by hospitals when they propose to construct or improve their facilities.

As federal funds became available to Ohio to establish health systems agencies, the MOHPF sprang into more significance when local funds were augmented by the federal support. Cook explained that the Columbus Hospital Federation actually changed its name to MOHPF in 1969. That group was soon concerned with interpreting needs, and gave advice about potential approval for any certificate of need. The actual certificate was to be awarded by the Director of Public Health, and it was difficult to build any new hospital without the relevant certificate. Decades earlier James, as he would write several times later, and with full agreement of the Columbus Cancer Clinic Board of Trustees, had decided to postpone all efforts to build a free standing cancer hospital until the need for more general hospital beds had been met. Members of MOHPF, along with many in the community, felt the issue in the 1970s was no longer more beds, but the tendency toward duplication, inefficiency, and rapidly rising costs.

LaBuhn, not without some support, took on the crusade to stop waste, and to halt the rush for a cancer hospital. He stated so, openly and repetitively, and to Wolfe. We can guess James' opinion, no, we need not guess, since he made it very clear. He spoke out for less, not more, regulation, and surely Republican Governor Rhodes espoused similar views. James said: "Competition has always improved service. Nowhere in this country have we said, 'If we limit the number of hotel beds the costs will come down.' What is so different about hospitals"? (60/8)

LaBuhn doubted the MOHPF would ever approve as many as 200 new beds in a community already considered by some to have a bed surplus. Cook wrote that LaBuhn's cocky style, combined with potential interference by bureaucrats, triggered a tirade by Wolfe who stated "nobody is going to stand in the way of a cancer hospital for Columbus." And if "John Walton" said that, then many would be sure it was correct. Skip Turner, M.C.P., now vice president for Managed Affairs at Mt. Carmel Hospitals, was present at the time decisions were made, and had ample chance later to hear Wolfe's opinions. Ultimately Rhodes actually did reject federal money linked to regulation, and at present a certificate of need is not required except for new nursing homes. Turner reports that in 1981: "The U. S. Congress passed legislation which permitted state governors to reject federal funding for Health Systems Agencies in their states. Governor Rhodes had his letter on President Ford's desk, rejecting funding for Ohio's HSAs, before the President had even received, much less signed, that legislation."

LaBuhn undoubtedly felt he was just doing his job, looking out for the community as a whole, but as a newcomer in town perhaps he did not sense he was facing a two decades long dream of more than one Columbus leader. James was forceful enough in his purposes, of course, but a wise man would have hesitated even more to disagree with Wolfe and Rhodes. Cook suggests, however, that neither tirade nor purity of purpose on either side was to end the controversy. Indeed, it was the major local controversy of the 1980s. Some suggest the issue is still not totally at rest and as recently as 2007, articles in *The Columbus Dispatch* reviewed once again discussion about the relative independence of the James Cancer Hospital from the rest of the University.

Eventually James had University President Enarson, Cramblett, Boards of Trustees of both the University and of the Columbus Cancer Clinic, Rhodes, the city's financial powers, and the Chamber of Commerce all on his side. For a time the MOHPF Board of Trustees, narrowly split, continued to resist in a vain attempt to keep health care expenditures under control. It was going to be expensive, very expensive, and payment might be problematic from patients with chronic cancer. The ultimate decision was never foreordained, indeed the Ohio Senate stripped the hospital from the capital improvements budget just before 1980. Do you assume even that setback stopped James, or his loyal lay colleagues? They seemed, in fact, to become more committed in the face of each obstacle.

On January 6, 1981, when James was clearly a member of the full time faculty at OSU, and the medical staff had become well aware of the real possibility of an eventual cancer hospital, Wolfe supplied his plane for another look at a major national cancer hospital, Memorial in New York City (65/2). On this trip major leaders from the OSU Hospitals were present: Judge Robert M. Duncan, chair of the Hospital Board, Charles Y. Lazarus, chair of the Facilities Committee for the Hospital Board, Arthur I. Vorys, of the University Hospital Board, Henry Cramblett, Vice President for Health Sciences, Donald A Cramp, executive director of University Hospitals, James, Dean

Jeffers, chief executive of Nationwide, Earl N. Metz, professor of Medicine and the elected chief of staff, and Manuel Tzagournis, dean of the College of Medicine. The group had only one busy day but did review aspects such as the rehabilitation program, a day unit for chemotherapy administration, uses of the cyclotron, and the optimal ways of collecting data. Probably the informal discussions were among the most useful aspects of the trip.

Money from the State Generates Success

In 1981, $40 million was approved by the Ohio Legislature to construct a twelve story cancer hospital on the OSU campus. This was preceded by a great deal of negotiating, Cook calls it "horse-trading," by legislators such as Harry Meshel, a particularly good friend of Tzagournis, and Mike Stinziano, and even very effective testimony on behalf of the hospital by Dean Cramblett himself. The sometimes hidden, but always powerful, hand of Rhodes, plus the reservoir of good will produced by years of service by James, by-passed all obstacles. Tzagournis and others had by then probably convinced James that an OSU base was needed if he was ever to get those millions of state money, but in fact in 1964 James had already written the hospital should be part of a teaching hospital complex (108/1). Leaders at OSU became convinced the hospital would come anyway, so let's just be sure it is ours. Adaptable, James who had held so long onto the concept of a free standing hospital, and who never gave up on the need for maximum autonomy, was eventually able to state it could become the best cancer hospital in America primarily because it is on the campus of a major university (142).

On June 9, 1981, in the *Dispatch,* Cramblett said MOHPF officials, presumably including LaBuhn, were lobbying behind his back against the hospital, using incomplete figures to suggest University Hospitals had a large percentage of unutilized beds, and that the cancer hospital was not truly needed (JC 150). On January 10, 1982, Cramblett, in the *Columbus Dispatch*, the paper always so remarkably supportive of the planned hospital, stated visiting groups who left from Columbus had found the two major national cancer hospitals so busy that they had to turn cancer patients away from the doors (JC 150). The *Dispatch* was not the only voice that echoed the dream. *The Columbus Citizen Journal* on May 25, 1982, quoted Rhodes: "It is not right that Ohioans must travel to Texas and elsewhere to seek advanced cancer treatment, not when we have the potential at Ohio State University for the finest cancer treatment center in the United States" (JC 150). On December 21, 1982, the University Hospital Board voted to support the planned cancer hospital, and suggested development of a clear plan of organization (95/17).

Complaints from some physicians in the community continued unabated and reverberated within the OSU administration. In response to such discussions and her concerns, James wrote Provost Ann Reynolds on January 15, 1982, that he estimated: "We will have 4,800 admissions to our 160 bed cancer hospital, 15-20% will come from our town, and the effort will not alter the cancer programs in the other hospitals" (120/9). He stated more than once that less than 10% of the patients at community hospitals were there because of cancer, and that no other hospital would suffer because of the cancer hospital.

Democratic Governor Richard Celeste, according to the *Columbus Dispatch* article on September 7, 1983, had "no special interest in building the hospital" (JC 150). Indeed the enthusiasm of people such as Wolfe may have been noted with no pleasure by the democratic governor. On December 1, 1983, the *Dispatch* added: "Is the hospital on hold?" and suggested that the reason for delay was that the hospital had moved low down in a new priority system within the Celeste administration (JC 150). The *Dispatch* headline on May 18, 1984, reads "Go for Cancer Hospital" after Celeste did finally release the appropriations (JC 150). Political efforts had continued and the key piece, state money, became available.

Long before 1983 it was obvious that James' passion for autonomy for the hospital had never lessened, but he probably was never really seeking complete isolation from OSU. He was, however, always seeking a hospital more than he was seeking recognition by the University. On September 21 the Ad Hoc Committee on Organization for the Ohio State Cancer Hospital recorded a resolution of the Board of Trustees: "Be it further resolved that the Board further recommends that an organizational plan be developed for the Cancer Institute Hospital so it can evolve with sufficient autonomy and independence governance so as most efficiently accomplish its mission and objectives." For a time, at least, it seems James had won.

Ground breaking

On July 10, 1984 ground was finally broken for the new hospital (50/2). In the same month James was appointed the first medical director for the hospital (122/7). In 1986 Tzagournis appointed James Chairman of the Task Force for Planning for the new hospital (114/10). In 1987 it was expected the facility would open as the year began. Although the chief OSU hospital administrator, Michael Covert, did attempt to subvert the effort (JC 95), an attempt was already underway to achieve diagnostic related groups (DRG) exemption. This would allow patients to be retained longer, if necessary, than was true in general hospitals. Such a ruling would both document autonomy and enhance chances of financial success.

On September 6, 1988, President Edward Jennings signed a letter with the approval of the Board of Trustees officially establishing the

Ground breaking for the Cancer Hospital (Medical Heritage Center, Arthur G. James, MD Collection)

On the occasion of hospital ground breaking. Dr. William Farrar, Dr. Katherine Clausen, Dr. Arthur James, Millie James, Norma Flesher, and Connie Jordan (Courtesy of Norma Flesher, RN)

cancer hospital. The governance of the new hospital was to be separate from University Hospitals with a reporting relationship to the Board of Trustees of OSU. It was President Jennings who announced at the dedication on September 11, 1987 that the cancer hospital was to be named the Arthur G. James Cancer Hospital and Research Institute in honor of James. President Jennings wrote in 2008:

> The naming of the building was first suggested by Len Immke and I and the board were enthusiastic about the suggestion. He of course was a pioneer in cancer surgery and worked very hard with the Governor and the legislature to obtain the funding. As I recall the building was first suggested in the late 70's, but the Ohio State administration was not in favor of giving the building a high priority what with the practice plan controversy. When I came on board that problem was behind us and thus supported the building particularly in view of the fact that it would advance the prestige of the university. Unfortunately the state budget was in terrible shape and the building was delayed again. The new governor was also not enthusiastic because it was a project of the previous governor. Eventually we prevailed but as you recall we had some extreme difficulty with the construction of the building and added university funds were required to complete the project. Recall the water pipe bursting on a very cold night.
>
> Administrative problems also got in the way of completing the building. Hospital administration wanted the James administration to report to the hospital director but the ACS insisted that it be a separate entity in order to receive grants. A separate entity prevailed, but not without much bureaucratic delays and unnecessary road blocks. Throughout, Art was a great help with the internal and external politicking

James in 1987 (Medical Heritage Center, Arthur G. James, MD Collection)

as well as assuring everyone with solid evidence that Ohio State could become a prime mover in research and care in national cancer work. In addition to his own work, that was one of his greatest contributions.

A letter from James to Immke on September 14, 1987 confirms President Jenning's recall: "I wanted to thank you in writing for your tremendous help in having the Cancer Hospital named for me. I was present at the Sheraton when you told the President that you thought the hospital should be so named, and I am sure you talked to him at other times, also. As I told you, I was completely surprised when the President made his announcement at the dedication. It is a tremendous honor, and I still can't believe it happened" (114/1).

On September 12, 1989 OSU Vice President for Health Affairs Tzagournis wrote the Ohio Director of Health to obtain certification and participation in Medicare programs, and to confirm the need for a highly desirable exception from DRG reimbursement to be in place immediately after certification by the Medicare officials. Some psychiatric units, hospitals for children, and rehabilitation facilities with long term and expensive care were eligible for such exemption. For "The James" to qualify, at least 80% of discharged patients had to have cancer, the hospital had to be free standing and not part of an acute-care facility, and the center had to conduct a certain amount of basic and applied research. *Business First* reported on February 11, 1991, that the exemption had finally been awarded and: "Cancer hospital gets waiver of price caps."

The issue of DRG exemption did not just die away. The *Dispatch* on May 4, 2008 reported that a planned expansion of the 160 to 288 beds threatened to lead to a loss of the exemption, because the guidelines under which "The James" originally had received its exemption had changed. The paper suggested the federal agency that

James with dedication plaque (Courtesy of Norma Flesher, RN)

James, President Jennings, David Thomas and Dean Tzagournis with architechural rendering of the hospital (Courtesy of The OSU Medical Center)

oversees Medicare had, after encouragement by local legislators, eventually moved to protect that valuable exemption. On June 16, 2008 "The James," which remained the only similar hospital in Ohio with a Medicare-reimbursement exemption, was again in the news. "James guarding Medicare exemption" the headline read, and the Cleveland Clinic was reported to be seeking a similar exemption. By late 1993 there were a total of nine cancer centers including M.D. Anderson and Memorial with exemptions similar to that of "The James," with no major additions since, but the future of these and other specialty hospitals, indeed of all non-profit hospitals, continues to be discussed by governmental groups including the Internal Revenue Service. Eternal vigilance is not just the price of liberty; vigilance is also needed to navigate the shifting federal guidelines, many established to promote social justice.

Last Minute Setback Before Opening

Tzagournis supplied a well written and detailed list of all that was being done to assure opening of the new cancer hospital facility. All seemed on track, opening was expected to be both smooth and proper. Proper it was; smooth it was not. In the wee hours of the night on December 18, 1989, a water line on the top floor froze and then burst sending water gushing throughout the building (142). 400,000 gallons of water flooded the building, and even the outside of the building was covered with sheets of ice. In fact the night was so cold that water mains in two other buildings on the University campus ruptured. (A brief effort, per Dennis Smith was made to protect James from the sight, but no one could fail to be aware of the dramatic event and the potential setback in the dream.) Amazingly, by 6:00 PM on the same day power had been restored and most of the free water was out of the building, but it would take time and money to complete the clean-up. The files include dozens of sympathy letters to James from all over the country. It was he who later referred to it as a "Baptism," but at the time of the accident no one smiled. In fact the structure of the building remained remarkably intact, and the cleanup left no evidence, but not until months and months later, and after a new expense of $2.4 million. The original contractor attempted to sue, but ultimately OSU collected $3 million in damages, and hired Smoot Associates to complete the construction (150/1). And finally, thank heavens, the first patient could be wheeled down the corridors by James himself on July 9, 1990.

Summary of the Obstacles to the Building of the Hospital

1) As we reviewed earlier, the rise of sub-specialization was not automatic. At the time James returned to Columbus as a surgical oncologist, not only he, but almost all other surgeons, operated in

James Cancer Hospital covered in ice (Medical Heritage Center, Arthur G. James, MD Collection)

multiple hospitals. Oncology as a separate discipline did not exist. He did not even focus exclusively on head and neck surgery for years, and many referring doctors would consider this part of the body a region for otolaryngologists anyway. So some may have wondered why follow this man who was proposing a gigantic new unit to treat all kinds of cancer.

Cancer Hospital admits first patient, Paul Proxmire, July 9, 1990 (Medical Heritage Center, Arthur G. James, MD Collection)

2) James accepted sooner than many in his generation the concept of sub-specialization in surgery. He felt cancer surgery of all kinds should be performed only by experts in cancer. Clearly there were general surgeons, dermatologists, gynecologists and otolaryngologists who did not agree.

3) Many of the administrators, and some of the doctors, believed that there was no purpose or need for a hospital just to treat cancer. There were beds on the wards that could be reassigned for cancer patients. Possibly, despite dozens of talks at which James insisted the impact of the special hospital would not hurt other practices or pocket books, many continued to suspect otherwise. According to Vincent, who was present when the Council of the Academy of Medicine refused to vote support for the cancer hospital, the issue was "the old town gown problems," jealousy of one group for another.

4) The fact that James wanted a free standing, autonomous, hospital seemed unwise to some, and unnecessary to others. It was held by many of the leaders at OSU that splintering off a section that was not devoted to the total academic enterprise might weaken the whole. The medical oncologists, with responsibility to teach students and residents, were understandably concerned that James would be more interested in "oncology fellows," narrowly focused on cancer, and as judged from his background fail to be fully aware of the academic needs of OSU as a whole. On May 5, 1986, Metz, professor of medicine, and perhaps the most widely respected internist and oncologist at OSU, wrote of concern: "[…] that it should conform to the administrative and academic structures which are in place lest it become an unwieldy giant in constant conflict with the teaching and patient care goals of the University Hospitals and the College of Medicine" (92/18). Ten days later his chairman, Mazzaferri, wrote to emphasizes that: "[…] the major cancer hospitals in this country do

not train internal medicine residents." He also had serious concerns regarding the planned autonomy, and stated his fear that oncology fellows, not internal medical residents, would be the ones trained.

It was not only the internists who felt uneasy about potentially autonomous programs. Norma Flesher reported the chair of the Surgery Department who succeeded Carey, Olga Jonasson, came to James' office to tell him she planned to fold oncology back into general surgery, discontinuing surgical oncology as a separate division. James vigorously, and effectively, demurred.

5) With the exception of the largely scorned psychiatric facility, Columbus Psychiatric Hospital, on the Hilltop west of Franklinton, and the tuberculosis unit at Alum Creek, there was little history in Columbus of specialty hospitals defined by disease (15). Saint Ann's Hospital on Bryden Road catered to women, and Children's Hospital on Livingston Avenue catered to children, but neither was designed to cover a single disease or specialty. The day of free-standing orthopedic hospitals and heart hospitals had not arrived in Columbus. That day arrived soon after the James Cancer Hospital.

6) James was tightly linked with the influential citizens of Columbus, a fact less impressive to academicians than to the laity. He maintained friendships, was generally sought when a citizen feared cancer, and was scrupulously professional and kind. Despite that success, perhaps because of it, there were some who accused him, behind his back, of being a "money doctor."

7) To the full time academic faculty James was not heavily identified with teaching students, although his schedule books certainly do contain many appointments to lecture. In addition, James had never been one of the primary teachers of students, and although we summarized his research, he was by no means a famous investigator. He was a practicing community-based surgeon. Until the 1970s, James never had a tenured university faculty position and his support seemed

more within the community at large than at OSU. After Carey invited him to take, and then James accepted, a named chair to establish the cancer division within the Department of Surgery, it became clear to everyone where his loyalties were most deeply planted (152/10).

That chair, which meant an endowment sufficient to pay his salary, was the "Lucius Wing Chair of Cancer Research and Therapy." Lucius A. Wing, M.D. was a surgeon and a 1903 graduate of OSU. His mother was the daughter of Professor Norton Townshend, a man very prominent in the early OSU faculty. Wing's other grandfather, also a Lucius, had been an OSU board member for almost twenty years. The money, $845,000, was from the estate of William H. Dickerson of Columbus, who was at OSU in 1904 and who wanted to establish a chair for research in cancer. $500,000 was used to establish the Lucius Wing chair in cancer, and the rest was committed to help establish an endowed Chair to honor the former dean, Richard Meiling.

8) There is no question, as was confirmed by Carey in 2008, that both Meiling and Zollinger did not want James at the University full time. Meiling and Zollinger were possibly the most prominent surgeons in Columbus, and were very concerned about the development of the OSU College of Medicine as a whole. Perhaps the single minded focus of James seemed to them a potential threat. The authors conclude, after dozens of interviews, that in fact James was exceptionally interested in his ties to the Medical Center, in its growth, and was deeply affectionate to OSU. A lesser man, or a more sensitive man, would have left and become full time at RMH by at least the mid 1970s. James himself said the biggest hurdles to getting the hospital were quite simply: "[…] convincing the community and the university, and then getting funding" (137/8).

"My personal goal is for this hospital to become number one in this country."

Arthur G. James, M.D.

Chapter 17
James Cancer Hospital Today: the dream lives on

The Hospital As Is, Compared to What James Foresaw

James talked to the Ohio State University Alumni on November 3, 1990 about "this tremendous cancer facility of ours." He did mean facility, not just hospital, with as much emphasis to be placed on research as on patient care. He was proud of the building itself, of course, and said two basic decisions had guided the architects in its construction: 1) "The architect should always 'keep the patient in mind'" and 2) "Programs and equipment would be 'state of the art,' always with the idea in mind of accomplishing more for the cancer patient and for each individual type of cancer than we are capable of doing for him now." He was able, now that most of the earlier uncertainties seemed resolved, at least at the time, to add the cancer hospital was 100% devoted to cancer research and care, all of its patients were cancer patients, and the staff devoted 100% of their time to cancer.

AirFare Magazine reported on the fifth anniversary of the hospital, July 9, 1995, that: "It has been named the ninth leading cancer treatment center out of 100 in the country by *Coping*, a national magazine for cancer survivors. Each year the hospital treats as many as 4,800 inpatients and nearly 75,000 outpatients from Ohio and around the world. The facility contains 268,000 square feet that include a radiation suite, 22 ambulatory chemotherapy suites, six operating rooms, 160 inpatient beds with 24 reserved for bone marrow transplantation, and 26 research beds." Numerous awards came to the new building, including a special meritorious award from the Ohio Hospital Association in 1992.

It will be, as of 2010, twenty years since the hospital became a real presence on The Ohio State University campus. Using the 2006-2007 *Annual Report of The Ohio State University Comprehensive Cancer Center – Arthur G. James Cancer Hospital and Richard J. Solove Research Institute*, it is possible to compare the dream of the Dreamer and the reality of the now.

Facilities: In 1963, James and Edgar Mansfield, President of Riverside Methodist Hospital, prepared plans for 29,000 square feet of space for patients, 29,000 square feet for research, and 30,000 square feet for a service area for both sections. The James now has 268,000 square feet on the primary 13 floors. Plans are underway for a dramatic increase beyond even that impressive figure.

James mentioned a facility to accommodate 100 patients in the 1960s (138/20); there are 160 licensed patient beds in the current hospital. There was, of course, no prediction of something that never existed at the time, a bone marrow transplant area, nor could James have foreseen the need for 40 examination rooms for the physicians, or the presence of chemotherapy units in at least five outpatient areas beyond The James itself. By 1994 over 500 bone marrow transplants had been performed.

In talk after talk, as he pushed the community toward the cancer hospital, James emphasized the desirability of radiation therapy in the operating rooms, as part of the fundamental ideas that he brought back from Memorial emphasizing multidisciplinary therapy and multispecialty consultation. There is, at the current hospital now, an intra-operative radiation therapy suite, gamma knife facilities for focusing radiation rays during stereotactic surgery, intensity modulated radio therapy, high dose brachytherapy, hyperthermia, and other radiation modalities that can be delivered intra-operatively.

Space: This more than equaled what James had projected over 30 years earlier. His earliest written plans mentioned only 20,000 to 30,000 square feet of space for patients, and a similar area for research. The annual report from The James for 2006-2007 now claims a total of 385,000 square feet, extending far beyond the original building.

Prior concerns: Obviously dozens of concerns could be mentioned, including the fact that all cancers are not cured. Payments systems, records, privacy concerns, competence with courtesy, and DRG exemption all remain topics for discussion. Essentially all patients are offered the chance to be on a research protocol, and almost monthly new chemotherapeutic agents and guidelines appear. Through the years it has become a common assumption, totally accepted, that the staff is essentially full time in The James. There is still, and perhaps always will be, some uncertainty regarding the meaning and extent of "autonomy" of The James. Some forces on campus would choose to divert receipts and efforts at The James toward other university goals. Cooperative efforts with other community hospitals are mixed at times with competition. The basic scientists may feel the clinicians have it easier to obtain time and money, or is it the other way around now, and the clinicians have come to feel like second class citizens. These are human issues, and we can expect such concerns to continue. The framework for cooperation, the quality of the facility and faculty, and the level of community acceptance, are all about as perfect as Dr. James, the ultimate perfectionist, would ever have imagined.

Patients: In 1982, in his letter to Provost Reynolds, James optimistically predicted there would be 4,800 patients per year, 80% or so from the local county and claimed again that the hospital would not weaken the other hospitals in Columbus. He probably would actually have been pleased with 4,000 patients per year as the hospital opened. In fact in the report for the year ending June 30, 2007, there were 8,307 inpatient admissions to The James. By 1996 there was 85% occupancy of the beds, and that, or a higher figure, continued every year thereafter. There were 182,014 visits to the outpatient areas in fiscal year 2006-2007.

If in the first years there were some "non-cancer" patient admissions, essentially everyone admitted to The James now is a person with cancer, and each one is a person the staff feels can be helped. Chemotherapy is being offered at The James, but now also at satellite facilities in Dublin, Ohio, on Kenny Road and at Ohio State University Hospitals East. The bone marrow transplant unit has continued, still with its total of 24 beds, and specialized radiation therapy units are linked to the six operating suites that are completely reserved for cancer patients. In view of his particular surgical skills, several of the specialized units would surely please James. Included are busy ones such as the maxillofacial suite and the program in dermatological cancer for melanoma victims. There are patient support programs including completely new efforts in palliative medicine. Occupancy of the hospital has recently hovered around 93%, and for several years the hospital has been "in the black." Indeed there now are active plans to add more beds and even more research!

Public service: James, as much as any faculty member at OSU, readily gave talks and educational presentations to local and state groups. That emphasis has continued with the current staff, particularly thanks to Drs. Schuller and Farrar, and the latter remains medical director of the Columbus Cancer Clinic. There have been special programs developed for women, as encouraging mammography, and a second mammography unit became necessary by 1994. Another area reminiscent of early efforts of James in community service is continued education to combat smoking, now forbidden on the entire medical campus. There have been efforts to develop a cancer telephone service for patient education, with over 20,000 calls by 1990, but there has been healthy competition in offering this service, and in fact in multiple other areas as well. The Ohio Cancer Information Service grant was awarded to West Virginia in 1992. In discussing the five year contract to run the Cancer Information Service, *Business First* on February 22, 1993 trumpeted: "OSU loss may be RMH gain."

Riverside Methodist Hospital (RMH) astutely labeled its unit for women's health "The Elizabeth Blackwell," the name of the first American woman physician, and an Ohio native. The James, not to be outdone, jointly with the American Cancer Society launched the Babe Zaharias Women's Cancer Center to honor the most famous woman golfer of all times, who died of cancer in 1956. Several post-operative rehabilitation programs are linked with the Zaharias Center.

Effect on other hospitals: Certainly James' prediction of adequate numbers of admissions was correct. Was he also correct to claim that the other hospitals were not going to be weakened, not going to be harmed, by the new cancer hospital? The authors happen to believe that an able competitor never hurts medical care, only an incompetent competitor is a threat to a place like The James. What do figures during the same time as those at OSU reveal about RMH, the hospital which is both the main clinical competitor; and the community hospital most involved with teaching students from the OSU Medical Center?

RMH in 2007 had over 100,000 admissions, diagnosed 2,500 new cancer patients, performed over 30% of the cancer surgery done in Columbus, and was ranked by *U. S. News and World Report* in 2004, 2005, and 2006 as one of the top cancer hospitals in America. Although OSU has a superb patient education program for cancer, RMH also has a very competitive phone information service and an elegant web site regarding cancer. It can be argued that not only did The James not hurt community efforts, it actually enhanced them.

James, along with other leaders of his time, was adamant about learning from registries of patients, and diagnostic types continue to be recorded and trends studied at any hospital that is serious about cancer care. One of the most common severe malignancies of males is prostate cancer. There were 521 new cases of prostate cancer studied at OSU and during the same time 330 at RMH.

Specific numbers are of value in national assessments, and although the OSU program in cancer is routinely listed nationally as the best in Ohio, the presence of The James Cancer Hospital served to raise awareness of the value of specialized care for all of central Ohio. Both Mt. Carmel Hospitals and RMH have much to be proud of, and both have benefited, not suffered, from the presence of The James Cancer Hospital at OSU that leads in both patient care and research.

Research: In the fifth year of the cancer hospital *AirFare Magazine* quoted James as saying: "The only way to improve our overall results in the effort to cure cancer is research. The only way to know if your research ideas are successful is to use them on patients and record the results." Research is the one area OSU must, and does, excel in when it is compared to any community hospital. Measurement of the value of research, sometimes called "metrics" by modern administrators, is difficult. Ideally the work should be judged later, and by its long term impact. Even that has become problematical; advances in science are incremental, halting, and reflect combined efforts; since modern research requires multiple people in multiple disciplines. It is impossible to list all, or even any substantial portion, of the over $115 million in research grants related to cancer awarded to the scientists representing twelve colleges within OSU. Cooperative linkages in cancer research extend widely across the campus of OSU, and now downtown to Children's Hospital as well.

We mentioned the need for basic scientists and clinicians to cooperate, a need particularly true at OSU, in contrast to the competing hospitals which have no significant basic science component. If there is residual tension between the basic scientists and the clinicians, it is more than offset by the joint grants and numerous planning and assessment committees involved in the cancer program as a whole, not as fragmented parts. The extent of cooperative research is nothing less than astounding. There are dozens of programs in cancer therapeutics, control, immunology, genetics of cancer, and even in viral oncogenetics – the study of viruses as causal factors in cancer. The latter seems very appropriate, particularly because James so often spoke of immunology. Recall that he was criticized for that controversial study on prisoners designed to test development of resistance to cancer.

Although James would have been proud of the work at The James in treating leukemia, the particular area of expertise of his dear friend Doan, and would have been intrigued by the work on retroviruses and on the effects of stress on disease, he might particularly welcome the current efforts that are akin to his own specialization when he was a local head and neck surgeon. The scientists and clinical surgeons at The James in 2007 studied and treated over 360 patients with cancer of the head and neck, and over 325 with malignant melanoma, both disorders James struggled against his entire professional life. There is even, among the hundreds of articles recently published from the research at The James, a formal research program to discover how doctors can be more effective in encouraging people to avoid smoking. Remember his repeated efforts to halt smoking at meetings and to educate the laity four decades earlier when he was president of the American Cancer Society. This list of his interests, as compared to what happens at present, could be endlessly extended in documentation. Not just that what goes around comes around, but the data offers unequivocal evidence that there is still work to be done. And that the modern James Cancer Hospital is doing it.

One of the issues mentioned several times in earlier chapters related to the potential difficulty of merging, mixing, fusing, or linking the James Cancer Hospital initiatives with the efforts of the Comprehensive Cancer Center (CCC). These programs are now one, at least in official name they have become one. Evolution has been ongoing, of course, and in 1992 the strategic plan suggested there was a common director but not a common policy making body (95/18). This has been addressed with more recent plans. The original designation of OSU as one of only 18 CCCs in the country was built on programs that existed at OSU even before 1976, and before James was full time at OSU. There are now 39 national CCCs. Ohio State continues to be classed as an "outstanding" one and therefore received $19.2 million from the National Cancer Institute for the current five years. More than 600 individual grants have been awarded to the more than 265 scientists who are part of the current effort at The James to treat and cure cancer. Even the often repeated wish of James that essentially every patient be included in a research protocol has been realized. This book is not primarily about the cancer hospital nor do we discuss the amazing research initiatives added since his time; but we are sure that he would be proud of both.

Development and fund raising: James developed another dream, to enhance fund raising on behalf of the hospital. That goal sometimes appeared even with his professional contacts, and he wrote a patient once: "I appreciate your letter but I would certainly not think of accepting your check....Of course I would have no way of stopping you if you would choose to make a charitable contribution to the Columbus Cancer Clinic, which, by the way, would be tax deductible."

The surgeon who had spent many hours developing plans for a hospital might in retirement have just pulled out a rocking chair and sat under that big fish from Canada mounted in his office. He might have even risen out of the rocker, from time to time, to show a school kid around "The James," usually referred to by him as "the hospital." Instead, in his last brief years he turned his attention to development. If there is one thing most medical professionals loathe, shun, and carefully leave to others, it is the requesting of funds. Physicians, on the average, are not the biggest donors, nor are they the most

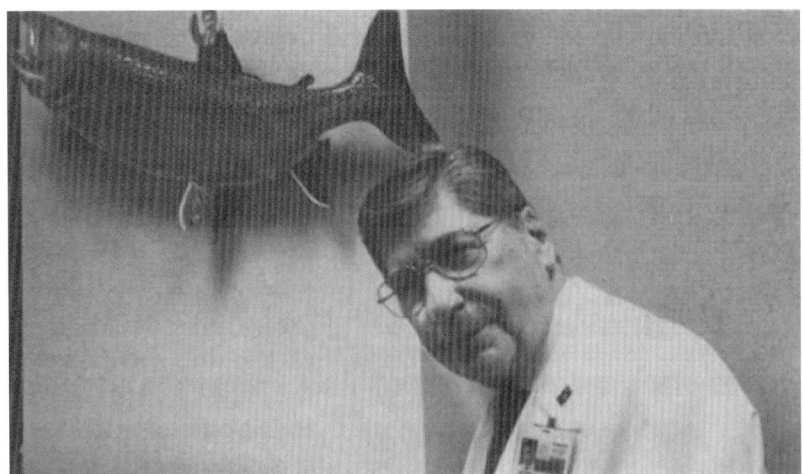

Art and Canadian catch (Medical Heritage Center, Arthur G. James, MD Collection)

enthusiastic of fund raisers. But in 1988 James asked to be made responsible to solicit funds for research and patient care (122/1).

Dr. Charles Meckstroth, who inserted the first cardiac pacemaker used in Columbus, remembered his last conversation with James:

> I was going to the parking lot and Art 'was going to work.' Art asked how I spent my time now that I was retired and was I enjoying life. I said that I had no problems filling time with snow skiing, water skiing, carving ducks and making wines and champagnes. Art said 'that's wonderful.' We parted after wishing each other the usual 'have a nice day.' Walking to my car I felt lucky to have great hobbies and knew that some retirees have none and therefore have problems with retirement, they have little to do all day long...I felt blessed that I did not have to continue like Art James. Then I started to think about the moment I had just experienced. I had just talked to one of the greatest surgeon-gentlemen ever to have been associated with our College of Medicine. Art James has pursued his goal of bringing to The Ohio State University a nationally known cancer hospital. This has been done in the face of politics, lack of money, hurt feelings, and the passage of time. Art could now be enjoying the 'fruits of retirement' with his wife and friends but instead he unselfishly works to finish the last details of the remarkable new institution that bears his name... On the way home to enjoy the bright spring morning, I felt very, very humble.

With experience nationally on behalf of the American Cancer Society and other groups that depended on the largess of the faithful, the committed, James had learned how to ask, how to receive, and how to get more. He had raised money for the United Way, for several national organizations, and for the Columbus Cancer Clinic (117/43).

He could be generous himself, no question about it, and he received an award from the Realtors Association that mentioned his generosity. He had long honed his recruitment skills when he helped the Columbus Cancer Clinic to acquire a board made up of affluent and committed citizens, and his recruits rewarded him and his causes.

He approached prior donors, beginning with those who had contributed to the Columbus Cancer Clinic. Several, including Dave Thomas and Len Immke, had already given substantial donations, in fact millions, but the money was to be used in the event of, and contingent on, construction of a free standing cancer hospital. His friend Richard Solove remained generous, even after the death of James. Some gave money specifically for research, as did the Schottenstein family with a gift of $2 million. Essentially all the members of the Board of the Clinic were contributors, but without money from the state there would never have been enough resources to build the hospital. The backing of the local newspaper and of the governor was crucial. And James more than any one person was responsible for such public and private backing. His affluent friends asked their friends to contribute because they trusted him and respected his goals. Many of the same names he relied on early appear later as members honored by induction into the "James Leadership Society."

James always hoped to raise money for a substantial endowment, a cushion to maintain and encourage growth (122/1). On November 7, 1988, he wrote Schuller, by then director of what James addressed in the letter as the "Cancer Hospital and Research Institute" and suggested: "[...] One of the most important requirements to making our CHRI a well known and top research center is a healthy endowment of $50 to $75 million and I believe this is within the realm of possibility [...] I would like to do this [...] and I believe there is no way I could benefit the CHRI more." James once supplied an outline of five pages naming potential donors, foundations, trusts, plans for recognition of all donors, and educational services aimed at encouraging all doctors and staff to be cognizant of the potential benefits of philanthropy for patient care and research.

By 2007 the endowment had achieved, not his $50 million, but $85 million. Current largess in gifts dwarfs anything he ever imagined. When he was still alive, but not totally well, in 1989-1990, over 900 individual gifts were received, for a total of over $2 million. In 2006-2007 over 33,000 gifts, and over $10 million in funds was given to support the program begun so much more modestly by that son of rural Ohio.

Attitudinal issues: It is somewhat presumptuous to end this chapter about the James Cancer Hospital with comments about attitude, or morale, or manner of delivering care. After all, neither author now works at the hospital and measurements are awkward, although all hospitals now try to assess approval ratings. Attitudes of staff and their activities are always a "moving target;" and it is hard to assume stability or constancy. However several things seem true. The community now, almost all of it, accepts the hospital with gratitude and pride. The feeling that it was not needed or would be harmful has largely passed. More relevant for this topic, almost anyone who has talked to several present or past patients at The James comment on the courtesy and kindness of the staff. We believe this is a real phenomenon, one academics and the larger community can be proud of. Why does that gentleness and kindness exist? 1) The patients are better known by the staff than is true on the general wards. 2) Families are often in evidence. 3) It is an uncommon employee who has not had an acquaintance or loved one touched by cancer. 4) Hospice, palliative care, education, and the lay press have encouraged awareness of the patient as a unique individual. 5) The facility is clean, the programs exciting, and the research is a cause for pride. 6) The senior staff, including Schuller, Smith, Farrar and oh-so-many others are overtly devoted to care that is compassionate as well as competent. 7) We like to think that the kindness and attentiveness to the needs of cancer patients that so many told us was typical of Dr. James remains a legacy as important to cherish as the dream edifice itself.

James in front of the completed Arthur G. James Cancer Hospital (Medical Heritage Center, Arthur G. James, MD Collection)

"I still like to get up early and go to the hospital, I see people whom I have treated or friends who are now patients of other doctors. I enjoy touring the hospital and discussing our research programs. I try to keep updated on new ideas."

Arthur G. James, M.D.

Chapter 18
Last Days: the Dreamer, but not the dream, comes to an end

Last Days, Joy and Sorrow

There was a steady stream of accolades, seminars, and dinner events in the later years of James' life, but these were never equal to the travels during his American Cancer Society days. His hectic surgical times were over as of 1989, and he officially retired on March 31, 1990 (117/33).

The sorrow of what he called the "baptism" of the James Cancer Hospital, when he grieved to see it covered by a sheet of frozen water, was long past, and his program was an unequivocal success. Funds for research seemed plentiful to an outsider, but of course never as plentiful as James felt was needed. He enjoyed leading tours, fishing in his farm pond, meeting with school children, and watching his skillful young protégés, men such as Drs. Farrar and Schuller, chair the meetings and treat the patients. He probably had more time for recreation: "Sports hold my interest and it takes a lot to make me miss an OSU football game, especially when the poor OSU 'Christians' are thrown to the University of Michigan 'Lions'" (JC 114).

James in 1994 (Medical Heritage Center, Arthur G. James, MD Collection)

For a time, not as long as many could have wished, he remained in his usual superb health, but not working his 12 hour days and no longer with duties on the weekend except for fund raising and leading tours of the hospital. He had had an uneventful hernia repair in 1966, a successful transurethral resection in 1976. There had been some respiratory problems, possibly bronchitis, earlier in his life (120/17). In 1961 he was transiently troubled, as are many in the Ohio Valley, with sinusitis (125/1). But overall he had really been a very healthy man (120/19).

In his later years Dr. Metz and others still saw him arrive very early in the day, just as the man who later became his dean, Tzagournis, had seen when Tzagournis was a student and resident. As had been true all of James' life, there were some disappointments and losses, including the failure to hire Gerald Murphy, M.D., and, according to Nurse Flesher, the inability to attract Judah Folkman to move to OSU from Harvard. James was very eager that Murphy, director of Roswell Park in Buffalo, be hired as director of the OSU Cancer Hospital. Murphy had published over 900 articles as peer reviewed papers; so many that some of the basic scientists at OSU questioned his true role in the publications. The Promotions and Tenure Committee of the College resisted hiring him, fearful of rumored political problems that might follow him from Buffalo. After the rejection, letters from James did help Murphy obtain other prominent positions in cancer centers, as well as offices in the national organizations in which James had once been so active.

A major sadness was the death of his vigorous younger colleague, John Peter Minton, M.D., Ph.D. Minton was a stalwart supporter of both James and of the oncology program, and had achieved a national image of his own. Minton was already on the scene when James was brought into the Medical Center to be full time chief of the Surgical Oncology Service. Minton had a prominent professional stature and a legendarily forceful personality, but by all reports worked quite cooperatively with James after he became the new colleague and boss. Minton was killed almost instantaneously while on the way to the hospital when, as he was stopped at a red light, his car was struck by a car driven by an epileptic having a seizure.

Minton and James (Medical Heritage Center, Arthur G. James, MD Collection)

Art and Millie with John P. and Jan Minton (Medical Heritage Center, Arthur G. James, MD Collection)

Other friends who had done so much to build the dream died one by one as the years rolled on. James' parents were long gone; his mentors all gone; and even the redoubtable Colonel Gardner that he had gone to Florida to visit when his former chief turned 90 had passed. James continued proud of his sons and loyal to the memory of school mates still alive in St. Clairsville, and he was a primary contact point for his old medical school class. With the passage of time, he sent many gentle letters of condolence and occasionally offered the eulogy at a funeral, as he did for his medical classmate David Dillahunt.

After Millie discovered quickly that she preferred to be closer to Upper Arlington than Worthington, where they briefly lived in a condominium, James and his beloved Millie moved into a double condominium on Mansion Way in Columbus. The home was not really one of a distinguished line of mansions, but it was very convenient and a pleasant place to live. His home was full of photographs, OSU athletic memorabilia, plaques, and special diplomas from the past. He maintained an office at the cancer hospital, and devoted much of his energy to raising money for the OSU development fund. The adaptable Norma continued as useful as ever, even if in a different role. A very elegant small dining room, the McCoy, near his office in the hospital made conferences and persuasion of donors more pleasant. And use of the room made the effort more successful. Together with Jack Havens, James had visited President John McCoy at the local bank and easily and quickly obtained the money to construct the room. In a sense The James Cancer Hospital had finally become a community project. Thanks to the Bernard Ruben family and the skill of Alfred Tibor, a statue of Hope appeared, and remains a symbol of the spirit of the Hospital that Hope graces.

Statue of Hope with Cancer Hospital (Medical Heritage Center, Arthur G. James, MD Collection)

Author Paulson is a neurologist who was well acquainted with James, as were most at the Medical Center, so it was no big surprise when James called to ask for a consultation "if you can spare the time." James had noted a tremor of his left hand, a tremor that was typical of the type noted in Parkinson's disease. The condition remained subtle, and without other features, but not for long, certainly not long enough. He began to develop a stoop in posture, slight imbalance, less spontaneity in his facial expression, and after less than a decade major difficulty with communication, then overt dementia. There is a progressive condition superficially like Parkinson's disease which is called Diffuse Lewy Body disease that he may have had. Medications that were helpful in modest degree for his Parkinsonian symptoms, and later for his mental state, never halted the inexorable decline toward total helplessness. Understandably, the public and friends sometimes labeled the condition as Alzheimer's, and indeed Diffuse Lewy Body disease can be similar to a combination of both Alzheimer's disease and Parkinson's disease. His decline grieved many and can be noted in later photographs; but he persisted in participating as long as he was able.

Millie and Art with Richard and La Donna Solove (Courtesy of James Family)

James had recurrence of the asthmatic like condition that reportedly troubled him in earlier years, congestive failure, developed problems with swallowing, and then needed around-the-clock care at all times. Millie was magnificent, as long her own health made it possible for her to help. The ever loyal Norma was there daily. The sons and daughter-in-law were helpful, almost daily visitors, and the family was able to hire devoted helpers for the couple they loved so much. His last days included frequent visits by Farrar, Schuller, Tzagournis, and others from the medical complex. He died on October 22, 2001, and had been unable to participate meaningfully in the hospital for several years before that. His Millie lived until 2004, and as she slowly declined Norma and sons David and Cameron and their families continued as faithful attendants.

James and his family on his 80th birthday (Courtesy of David James)

Several memorial ceremonies at the OSU Medical Center and in the community were enriched by the audio visual work of son Cameron, an expert in that field, and numerous publications expressed grief that James was no longer leader, spokesman, and eternal optimist in the battle to cure cancer. Yes, James was gone, but several during the eulogies commented on the success of his Dream for a Cancer Hospital. That Dream is, in fact, more vitally alive than ever.

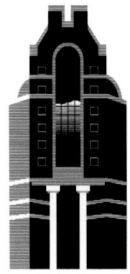

"In making early morning patient rounds, I usually pass a large window through which I can see the construction site. On a morning when the sun is just beginning to rise, the Institute makes a very impressive picture.
It is obvious that a new day is dawning."

Arthur G. James, M.D.

Conclusions and What We Learned from James' Life and Dream

As we review a meaningful life the accomplishments may seem inevitable, foreordained, but that is only true in retrospect. If it is true that much of our fate is not due to the stars but due to ourselves, then the characteristics of a life like that of James can be lifted up to illuminate reasons for success. The hope for such lessons, with the story of his dream, is what we intended to offer with our tribute to Dr. Arthur G. James. Why was he who he was?

James inherited a good brain, optimism, and physical vigor from his ancestors. His parents set an example of sobriety, reliability, and hard work. His virtues were classic midwestern ones, as was true even of his understated manner.

The magnificent land grant university, OSU, offered financial assistance, mentoring, and the promise of continued growth. He chose from among the best as he sought advanced medical training at the universities of Ohio State, Chicago, and Duke, and fellowship at Memorial Hospital.

He not only had remarkable mentors, he adhered to their example, and was comfortable cultivating their friendship.

All his life he was responsive to others. He was quick to write thanks, careful when offering advice, genial to all, and loyal to friends. His voice was soft, his handshake was gentle, and he shunned overt conflict. Those who did not feel warm toward him still held him in respect, and disagreements usually reflected different opinions about the role of a hospital such as The James.

He never hesitated to be a committee member, or an officer, and he held onto any position that might prove advantageous.

He was not hesitant to join, even to "stroke," the elite and the wealthy, nor was he sheepish about asking for their help. He not only was kind to patients, he often became their friend.

He was blessed with the help of three remarkable women, his mother Rosa, his devoted wife Mildred, and the ever loyal nurse Norma.

He was sustained by that bright dream, his lifetime goal. He thought nobly, and "dreamed big," but he always "focused small," with careful attention to the patient at hand, the committee he chaired, and the immediate issues he faced.

Lastly, and perhaps the real key to it all, he was a fine doctor. The physicians remembered most through the ages are not the scientists in the laboratory. The ones most of us remember are our personal physicians, the ones who taught patient care, and the ones who showed concern for the patient above all else. Dr. Arthur G. James was a worthy member of the fraternity of those entitled to be called "the Good Doctor."

References

Arthur G. James, MD Collection, Spec.200502.James, John A. Prior Health Sciences Library, Medical Heritage Center, The Ohio State University.

Barth, R. F., et. al. "Boron Neutron Capture Therapy of Cancer: Current Status and Future Prospects." <u>Clinical Cancer Research</u> 11(2005): 3987-4002.

Bliss, Michael. <u>William Osler: a Life in Medicine</u>. Philadelphia: Oxford University Press, 1999.

Crile, George. <u>George Crile, An Autobiography</u>. Philadelphia: Lippincott, 1947.

Flesher, Norma. Personal Interview. 2008.

Greenwald, Marilyn S. <u>A Woman of the Times: Journalism, Feminism, and the Career of Charlotte Curtis</u>. Athens: Ohio University Press, 1999.

Interview with Dr. Richard Meiling Conducted by Dr. Robert Sutton on November 21, 1983, The Ohio State University Archives.

Jacobs, Clara. Personal Interview. 2008.

James, Cameron D. Personal Interview. 2008.

James, David A. Personal Interview. 2008.

Mallon, William J. *Ernest Amory Codman: The End Result of a Life in Medicine*. Philadelphia: Saunders, 2000.

Mayo, Charles W. *Mayo: The Story of My Family and My Career*. Garden City: Doubleday Press, 1968.

Moreno, Jonathan D. *Undue Risk: Secret State Experiments on Humans*. New York: W. H. Freeman, 2000.

The Ohio State University, Comprehensive Cancer Center and Arthur G. James Cancer Hospital and Richard J. Solove Research Institute. *Annual Report*. Columbus: The Ohio State University, 2007.

Paulson, George W. *An Extraordinary Surgeon: James Fairchild Baldwin, M.D. 1850-1936*. Columbus: Medical Heritage Center, 2005.

—. *The Ohio State University College of Medicine. Volume III, 1998.* Columbus: Ohio State University, 1998.

Paulson, George W., and Marion E. Sherman. *Hilltop: A Place and a Sanctuary for Healing, Its Past and Its Future*. Fremont: Lesher Printers, 2008.

Time The Weekly Newsmagazine. XVII.2 (1931).

Underwood, Paul. *The Enarson Years, 1972-1981*. Columbus: The Ohio State University, 1985.

Wilds, John, and Ira Harkey. *Alton Ochsner, Surgeon of the South*. Baton Rouge: Louisiana State University Press, 1990.

Wooley, Charles, and Barbara Van Brimmer. <u>John Howell Janeway Upham, M.D., 1871-1960: The Survival Years</u>. Columbus: Medical Heritage Center, 2003.

—. <u>The Second Blessing: Columbus Medicine and Health The Early Years</u>. South Egremont: Science International Corporation, 2006.

James Collection Summary

Medical Heritage Center
The Ohio State University
Prior Health Sciences Library
376 W. 10th Ave.
Columbus, OH 43210

Arthur G. James, MD Collection
Spec.200502.James
165 linear feet, 1923 – 2002

INTRODUCTION

Access

The collection is open to the public and is available for viewing during the hours that the Medical Heritage Center is open to the public (1-5PM, Monday-Friday) or by appointment. Materials do not circulate and must be used in the supervised reading room.

Some materials in the collection are restricted to protect privacy rights. They are designated "RESTRICTED" in the finding aid and on the file folder. Please see the Medical Heritage Center curator for assistance with restricted files.

Other restrictions, including copyright, may exist and some materials may be too fragile to photocopy or digitize. The MHC charges for duplication services, which must be performed by staff.

Citation

[Identification of item], Arthur G. James, MD Collection, Spec.200502.James, John A. Prior Health Sciences Library, Medical Heritage Center, The Ohio State University.

Processing Notes

Journals and books relating to The Ohio State University and the topic of cancer were included in the James donation. These journals and books were removed from the collection and, where appropriate, placed within the general holdings of the Medical Heritage Center and the Prior Health Sciences Library. A bibliography of the books has been added to appendix A of this finding aid.

Slide additions, boxes 160 – 165, were added to the collection April 2008.

Date accessioned: 2005
Date processing began: September 2006
Date completed: October 2007
Date of additions: April 2008

Property Rights

The Ohio State University Medical Heritage Center owns the property rights to the Arthur G. James, MD Collection.

Donors

The Arthur G. James, MD Collection was donated to the Medical Heritage Center in 2005 by Cameron and David James, Arthur James' sons.

Personnel

Kristin Rodgers, MLIS served as the collection's archivist and began processing in September 2006. Rodgers completed the project in October 2007.

Research Restrictions

Restricted folders are noted in the finding aid and on the file folder. Restricted items include named patient medical information. See the Medical Heritage Center curator for assistance with restricted folders.

Arrangement of the Collection
Organization:

Before arriving at the Medical Heritage Center, the James Collection was organized by Norma Flesher, RN, Dr. James' longtime nurse–secretary, and where appropriate that order was maintained.

Each box of materials has been assigned a number.

Series Listing:

Series I: Artifacts, Artwork, and Oversized

Series II: Associations/Foundations/Societies

Series III: Awards and Memorials

Series IV: Cancer Hospital Research Institute (CHRI)

Series V: Correspondence

Series VI: Media

Series VII: Personal

Series VIII: Publications

Series IX: Research

Related Collections

Related collections *within* the Medical Heritage Center include:

- § The William G. Myers, MD, PhD Collection as Dr. Myers was a longtime friend and colleague of Dr. James (they met in September 1930 as first year premedical students at OSU); and, Myers was also involved in helping to secure funds to build the Arthur G. James Cancer Hospital and Richard J. Solove Research Institute at The Ohio State University.
- § The Robert M. Zollinger, MD Collection as Dr. Zollinger and Dr. James were colleagues.

SCOPE AND CONTENT NOTE

Scope and Contents:

The Arthur G. James, MD Collection (approximately 165 linear feet) consists of artifacts, awards, slides, negatives, photographs, audio and video recordings, as well as various papers related to associations and departmental records, correspondence, and publications. These items document his position as the first medical director of the cancer hospital, his thirty-five year effort to acquire funding to build a cancer hospital in central Ohio, his presidential year with the American Cancer Society, his career at the Ohio State University, and his family life.

People of note in this collection include: William Farrar, MD; William G. Myers, MD; Vernal Riffe, former speaker of the Ohio House of Representatives; R. David Thomas, Founder of Wendy's International, Inc.; and George Voinovich, United States Senator.

- Central Surgical Association
- The Cleveland Clinic Foundation
- Columbus Board of Realtors
- Columbus Cancer Clinic
- The Columbus Club of Printing House Craftsmen
- The Columbus Foundation
- Columbus Jewish Foundation
- Columbus Rotary Club
- Combined Meeting: American Society for Head and Neck Surgery (ASHNS) & Society of Head and Neck Surgeons (SHNS)
- Combined Meeting: The Society of Surgical Oncology (SSO) & The Society of Head and Neck Surgeons (SHNS)
- Department of Health, State of Ohio
- European School of Oncology
- General Motors Cancer Research Foundation, Inc.
- Golden Key National Honor Society
- H. Lee Moffitt Cancer Center and Research Institute, University of South Florida
- Hamilton County Health Department
- Horatio Alger Association of Distinguished Americans, Inc.
- Howard Hughes Medical Institute
- The Hubert H. Humphrey Cancer Research Center
- Ingram-White Castle Foundation
- International Academy of Oncology, General Surgery Section, American Chapter
- International Union Against Cancer (UICC)
- The Junior League of Columbus, Ohio, Inc.
- Kenneth Norris Jr. Comprehensive Cancer Center/Cancer Hospital, University of Southern California

JAMES COLLECTION SUMMARY

- The Kresge Foundation
- Landacre Society, The Honorary Scholastic and Research Society of the Ohio State University College of Medicine
- Lions Club of Columbus
- Marie Curie Memorial Foundation
- Medical Forum
- Memorial Sloan-Kettering Cancer Center
- The National Cancer Institute
- Ohio Hospital Association
- The Ohio State University
- Order of Hippocrates
- Pi Lambda Theta, Central Ohio Chapter
- The Presidents Club, The Ohio State University
- The Robert M. Zollinger Ohio State University Surgical Society
- Rocky Mountain Cancer Conference
- Societe Internationale de Chirurgie
- The Society of Surgical Oncology (founded as James Ewing Society)
- The Society of Head and Neck Surgeons
- St. Clairsville Alumni Association
- St. John the Baptist Catholic Church and Italian Cultural Center
- State Medical Board of Ohio
- Toledo Surgical Society
- Torch Club
- United Commercial Travelers of America
- United Way of Franklin County
- University of Colorado, Department of Surgery

- o   The University of Texas MD Anderson Cancer Center (MD Anderson)
- o   Wendy's International, Inc.
- o   Woman's Auxiliary to the Ohio State Medical Association

Items of note in this series include: Box 54 which contains materials about Dr. James' year as president of the American Cancer Society.

Series III: Awards/Memorials (8 boxes) contains awards, certificates, plaques, and statues given to James for his achievements by various organizations throughout his lifetime.

The items in this series are arranged into 4 subseries:
- o   Certificates (1 box)
- o   Framed (2 boxes)
- o   Plaques (3 boxes)
- o   Statues (2 boxes)

Series IV: Cancer Hospital Research Institute (16 boxes) contains material relating to all aspects of the Arthur G. James Cancer Hospital and Richard J. Solove Research Institute. The records are of hospital equipment; general information about or from the hospital; and, various committee meeting minutes.

The items in this series are arranged into four subseries:
- o   Equipment (2 boxes)
- o   Foundation and Development (6 boxes)
- o   General (5 boxes)
- o   People (3 boxes)

Series V: Correspondence (21 boxes) contains letters and memorandums mostly to or from Dr. James. The series has been arranged alphabetically by last name of the sender or receiver (whichever person was not Dr. James). When three or more pieces of correspondence belonged to the same individual a folder was created for that person. Each letter of the alphabet – except X which had no correspondence – also contains a general folder that holds all of the correspondence for that letter from individuals with less than three pieces of correspondence. The correspondence in these folders is also arranged alphabetically.

Series VI: Media (16 boxes) contains boxes of audio and video records, photographs, scrapbooks and slides.

The items in this series are arranged into three subseries:
- o Audio and Video Recordings (4 boxes)
- o Photographs
    - o Buildings (1 box)
    - o Groups (2 boxes)
    - o James & Family (1 box)
    - o Scrapbooks
- o Slides (8 boxes)

The Audio and Video Recordings are dated according to when the recording was made (i.e. their airdate in the case of video recordings).

Mildred James made each scrapbook which documents various aspects of Dr. and Mrs. James life. Each scrapbook is boxed individually and due to their oversized nature is listed under Series I: Artifacts, Artworks and Oversized.

Boxes 160 – 165 of slides were added in April 2008. These slides were kept in the original order received and are numbered according to the slide tray number in which they were found. For example, item 1 in box 164 is called 29 as that was what is written on the slide tray.

Series VII: Personal (8 boxes) contains material of a more personal nature related to James' life.

The items in this series are arranged into five subseries:
- o   Dr. Arthur James (1/2 box)
- o   Family (1/2 box)
- o   Talks (6 boxes)
- o   Travel (1/2 box)
- o   Work (1/2 box)

All subseries in this category are arranged alphabetically except "Talks" which is arranged chronologically.

Because they are small in size, the subseries "Dr. Arthur James" and "Family" are boxed together; and, the subseries "Travel" and "Work" are boxed together.

Within the "Talks" subseries there is a box named "Talks – Incomplete Talks" which is comprised of talks given by Dr. James that are missing one or more note cards of each speech, in some cases there is only one note card for a speech as the others are missing. In these situations the card number has been recorded in the container listing.

Series VIII: Publications (5 boxes) contains CHRI publications, James' writings, and newspaper clippings about Dr. James and the cancer hospital.

The items in this series are arranged into 3 subseries:
- o   Cancer Hospital Research Institute (1 box)
- o   James' Writings (3 boxes)
- o   Newspaper Clippings (1 box)

Series IX: Research (9 boxes) contains material relating to James' Research and his OR and schedule books.

The items in this series are arranged into one subseries:
- o   James' Research (9 boxes)

Items of note in this series are Dr. James' OR and Schedule Books.

CONTAINER LISTING of all 165 boxes is available from the Medical Heritage Center and the collection can be viewed during their public hours of 1-5pm, Monday – Friday, or by appointment.

Acknowledgements

Particular thanks are due to the James family, and to Norma Flesher.

The following persons, in addition to those thanked in the preface, read part, or all, of this manuscript, sent information, supplied photos, offered opinions or recollections, appeared in letters in the James collection, or were just helpful in encouraging the project. None are responsible for our errors, of course, and we are grateful to them all. They are listed alphabetically and without titles, and because of the widespread encouragement of our efforts it is probable that we overlooked some individuals. One of the rewards of the project was the chance to make contact with so many helpful people.

Abel, Robert; Barker, Ray; Barth, Rolf; Benedetti, Constantino; Boles, Thomas; Bonta, Marco; Burnham, John; Christoforidis, A.J. and Anna; Clausen, Kathryn; Cornwell, David; Covert, Michael; Cramblett, Henry; Ellison, E. Christopher; Farrar, William; Flesher, Norma; Gahbauer, Reinhard; Gee, E. Gordon; Gibson, Adeline; Gilbert, Ivan; Glaser, Ronald; Goodman, Joseph; Grever, Michael; Hardymon, Ellen; Havens, John; Immke, Charlotte; Jacobs, Clara; James, Cameron; James, David; Jennings, Edward; Johnson, Ernest; Kakos, Gerald; Kramer, John; Kuhn, Al; McNealey, Jeff; Meckstroth, Charles; Meiling, George; Metz, Earl; Metzger, Paul; Newton, William; Nichols, James; Olsen, John; Paulson, Ruth; Peppe, Mike; Pollock, Jessie; Pontious, Bruce; Saunders, William; Scanlon, Mike; Schuller, David; Shkurti, William; Smith, Dennis; Soloway, Albert; St. Pierre, Ronald; Turner, Skip; Tzagournis, Manuel; Vincent, Donald; Wall, Michael; Weis, Lawrence; Wheeler, Warren; Wiener, Judy; and Yohn, David.

Index

1607 Neil Avenue: 67, 68, 69, 71, 133, 142, 143

8th Air Force: 36, 39, 40

65th General Hospital (Army): 34-36, 38-41, 153, 215

Airfare magazine: 183, 188

Allied Medicine Program: 82

Alpha Omega Alpha, honorary society: 149

Alum Creek Reservoir: 144

Alzheimer's disease: 14, 83, 202

American Board of Surgery: 35

American Cancer Society (ACS) and its committees: 61, 72, 74, 93, 97-106, 108-112, 116, 118, 121, 131, 132, 145, 149, 152, 173, 187, 190, 192, 196, 213, 215, 218

American College of Surgeons: 35

American Federation of Clinical Oncology Societies: 50, 215

American Journal of Surgery: 101

American Society of Hematology: 61

American Thyroid Association: 80

Anderson, H., Academy of Medicine: 157, 164, 181

Annual reports: 184, 185, 208

Antrim, Ohio: 44

Appearances before congressional committees of Senate or House: 105

ArtMil Acres: 144

Aspiration biopsy: 118

Babe Zaharias Woman's Cancer Center: 187

Baldwin, J.: vii, 79-81, 91, 208

Barker, R.: 142, 222

Barnes, A.: 53

Barth, R.: 114, 207, 222

Belmont County: 1, 5, 7, 14-15, 108

Ben Franklin Hospital: 156

Benedetti, C.: 92, 222

Berman, H.: 84

Bethel Road: 144

Black Hand Gang: 2

Black, C.:80, 90
Blackford, J.: 94
Block memorial lecture: 132
Bologna, Italy: 104
Bonta, J.: 71-73, 100, 124, 131, 222
Brown, I.: 35, 36
Brunschwig, A.: 26, 46
Buckeye:17, 123
Burnham, J.: viii, 222
Burst pipe: 173, 178
Cancer Information Services: 187
Cancer Prognosis manual: 118
Carey, L.: 73, 76, 77, 78, 82, 86, 126, 181, 182
Catholic Church: 10, 11, 152, 217
Celeste, R.: 170, 171
Ceramic Drive: 89, 90
Christoforidis, A.: 68, 106, 114, 222
Citizen Journal: 148, 170
City of Hope Medical Center: 84
Clark, Lee: 164
Clouse, G.: 159
Coal mines: 2, 4, 5-7, 15, 151
Codman, E.: vi, 208
Columbus Cancer Clinic: 61, 79, 81, 82, 87, 88, 90, 101, 108, 119, 132, 136, 140, 156-160, 162-164, 166, 168, 187, 191-193, 215, 216
Columbus Dispatch: 87, 101, 120, 148, 155, 157, 162, 168, 170
Columbus Monthly: 164
Commando procedure: 119, 124, 155
Comprehensive Cancer Center: 105, 157-159, 184, 190, 208, 216
Cook, H.: 162, 164, 166-169
Coping: 183
Covert, M.: 171, 222
Crabapple Mine: 6
Cramblett, H.: 77, 162, 163, 168-170, 222
Cramp, D.: 168

Crile, George: vi, 207
Crile, George Jr.: 119, 120
Curtis, C.: 22, 207
Curtis, G.: 21, 22, 25, 118
Curtis, L.: 22
Cutler, E.: 54
Cyclotron: 113, 169
Daniels, Miss: 8
Diffuse Lewy Body Disease: 202
Dillahunt, D.: 18, 200
Doan, C.: 47, 53-56, 58-62, 65, 81-84, 88, 91, 118, 132, 140, 189
Dodd, V: 20, 21, 25, 65
Donors: 63, 93, 96, 101, 140, 144, 191, 193, 194, 200, 211
Douglas, J.: 43
DRG, medicare exemption: 171, 175, 185
Duke and Duke University: 27, 34, 35, 40, 41, 104, 116, 117, 132, 136, 205
Duncan, R.: 168
Eisenhower, D: 39
Ellis Island: 2, 5
Ellison, E. C.: 86, 222
Ellison, E. H.: 55
Enarson, H.: 81, 163, 168, 208
Ewing J.: 48
Farber, D.: 109
Farms: 143, 144, 147
Farrar, W.: 77, 91-93, 172, 187, 195, 196, 203, 213, 222
Fawcett, N.: 81
Fishing: 30, 101, 144, 145, 196
Flesher, N., (Norma): viii, 68-70, 149, 172, 181, 198, 207, 212, 222
Florida Keys and Islamorada: 40, 101, 145, 200
Folkman, J.: 90, 132, 198
Fort Bragg: 35
Fort Devers: 35
Frajola W.: 60, 118, 140
Fulton, W.: 15, 16

Gahbauer, R.: 68, 113, 222
Gardner, C.: 38, 40, 41, 200
General Motors Sloan Cancer Research Award: 85
Germany: 2, 36, 38, 56, 57
Giangiacomo, A.: 1-3, 6, 7, 14, 15, 28, 39
Gilbert, I: 91, 140, 222
Hadassah Myrtle Wreath Award: 90
Harding H.: 94
Hardymon, E.: 131, 222
Hatcher's Cafeteria: 16
Havens, J.: 145, 147, 151, 162, 164, 200, 222
Hayes, W: 93
Hays, W.: 12, 14, 15, 151
Health Systems Agencies: 166, 167
Henschke, U.: 114, 132
Hiram College: 58
Horatio Alger Award and Horatio Alger: 149-152, 215, 216
Hospital Commission and Columbus Hospital Federation: 156, 166
House of Lords, and trip to England: 108
Hunt, W.: 22
Inglis, W.: 94
Institutional Review Boards (IRB): 121
Italian Festival: 149, 152, 153, 215
Jacobs, C.: viii, 2, 5, 10, 11, 207, 222
James, C.: viii, 31, 32, 65, 99, 203, 207, 211, 222
James, D.: viii, 7, 31, 32, 39, 40, 143, 147, 203, 207, 211, 222
James, F.: 7, 8, 10, 16, 17, 145
James, L.: 26
James Ewing Society: 49, 109, 217
Jennings, E.: 64, 171, 173, 177, 222
Jonasson, O.: 77, 181
Kakos, G.: 126-128, 222
Kennedy, T.: 104
Kettering, C.: 43
Kinsey, D.: 72

Kinsman Hall: 81
Krebiozin: 113
L'Aquila of Abbruzzo: 2, 4
LaBuhn, G.: 135, 166, 167, 169
Lazarus, C.: 151, 162, 168
LifeCare Alliance: 80, 90
Lucius Wing Chair of Cancer Research and Therapy: 26
Lucy Wortham James Award: 26, 109, 149
Lumpectomy: 119, 120
Maennerchor: 95
Kelly, D.: 94
Mallory, T.: 94
Mammography: 90, 103, 109, 116, 119, 187
Mansfield, E.: 89, 156, 184
Marie Curie Memorial Foundation: 44, 108, 217
Markee, J.: 117
Marsilid: 113
Martin, H.: 43, 44, 49
Mattingly, C.: 94
Mattison, T.: 129
Mayo Brothers: vi, 208
Mazzaferri, E.: 80, 180
Meckstroth, C.: 20, 22, 192, 222
Medical Director: 61, 63, 81, 84, 87, 92, 93, 171, 187, 213
Medical Forum: 94, 95, 217
Medical Heritage Center (MHC): v, vii, 207-213, 221
Medical Review: 94
Medical Symposium: 94
Meiling, R.: 25, 56-58, 62, 77, 81-84, 182, 207, 222
Memorial Hospital (Sloan-Kettering):34, 42-46, 48-50, 65, 66, 68, 71, 84, 119, 120, 129, 132, 142, 155, 156, 159, 168, 186, 205, 215, 217
Meshel, H.: 169
Metz, E.:169, 180, 198, 222
Metzger, P.: 164, 222
Mid Ohio Health Planning Federation (MOHPF): 157, 166-169

Minnick, T.: viii
Moulton, E.: 131
Murphy, G.: 198
Mussolini, B.: 14
Myers, W.: 106, 114, 115, 132, 213
National Cancer Institute (NCI): 105, 157, 158, 190, 217
National Chemotherapy Conference: 103
Nelson, S.: 131
Neoprobe: 113
News and Observer: 38
Newton Hall: 67
Nixon, R., and war on cancer: 157
North Carolina: 27, 35, 39, 104
North wing of University Hospital: 81-83
Oak Ridge: 114
Ochsner, A.: vi, 208
Ohio Medical Education Network (OMEN): 58
Ohio State Medical Association (OSMA): 58, 83, 218
Ohio State University, The; OSU: vii, 1, 7, 15, 47, 52, 79, 110, 163, 170, 183, 184, 186, 192, 207, 208, 210, 211, 213, 217
Ohio Veterans Hall: 153
Olentangy River Road: 12, 71, 74, 88, 113, 142, 144
Oncology: 44, 46, 49-51, 61, 68, 72, 76, 77, 82, 103, 105, 114, 117, 140, 158, 164, 179-181, 198, 215-217, 223
Onna: 2, 4, 5
Osler, W.: vi, 48, 207
OSU Medical School: 17, 22
College of Medicine, etc.: 18, 34, 52, 54, 56, 57, 60, 81-84, 158, 162, 163, 169, 180, 182, 192, 208, 217
OSU Stone Laboratories: 140
OSU University Hospitals: 22, 27, 35, 56, 60, 62, 65, 66, 68, 69, 73, 75, 77, 81-83, 85, 94, 121, 126, 152, 163, 168-171, 173, 181, 187
OSU University Hospitals Board: 168, 170
Pack, G.: 44-47
Papanicolaou, G.: 109, 132

INDEX

Pataskala: 144

Paugh, A.: 80, 84

Peabody, F.: 59

Peale, N.: 150

Pezzopane, R.: 2

Piave Society: 152

Pollock, J.: 12, 222

Presbyterian Church: 11

Prisoners, experiments on: 120, 121, 189

Prostate cancer: 114, 188

Pugh, D.: 157

Pyroscan: 115

Queen Mary Ocean Liner: 36

Radical neck surgery: 124

Rand vaccine: 112

Rays: 89, 90, 185

Research: vi, vii, 14, 20, 21, 26, 35, 42, 48, 50, 59, 60, 64, 75, 79, 82, 85, 89, 94, 105, 108-121, 123, 132, 139, 142, 152, 156-159, 164, 175, 181-191, 193, 194, 196, 207, 208, 212, 221

Reynolds, A.: 170, 186

Riffe, V.: 135, 164, 165, 213

Riverside Methodist Hospital, RMH: 56, 62, 73, 74, 88, 89, 101, 156, 184, 187

Robson, A.: 12

Rockefeller, J.: 42

Round Table of the Medical Arts: (ROMA): 94

Ruben, B.: 201

Ryan, M.: 40

Sabin, F.: 60

Saunders, W.: 51, 64, 222

Scanlon, M.: 145, 147, 222

Scarlett, M.: 89

Schottenstein family: 193

Schuller, D.: 51, 63, 64, 86, 128, 187, 193, 195, 196, 203, 222

Shannon, J.: 14

Siblings of Dr. James: viii, 8, 10, 16, 17, 28, 145

Sloan, A.: 43
Smith W.: 160
Smith, D.: 128, 178, 195, 222
Smith, T.: 24
Society of Head and Neck Surgeons: 49, 50, 215-217
Solove, R.: 133-136, 162, 164, 193, 202
Somalia: 2
Southam, C.: 120
Southwestern Oncology Group (SWOG): 117
Spaatz, C.: 39
Spaghetti: 6, 152, 153
Spam: 14
St. Clairsville: 5, 7, 8, 12, 15, 16, 44, 131, 200, 217
St. John the Baptist Church: 149, 152, 215, 217
Starling-Loving Hospital: 19, 23
Stinziano, M.: 169
Silvia, Queen of Sweden: 132
Task Force for Planning: 171
Temperature for diagnosis: 115, 116
Theta Kappa Psi: 18, 19
Thomas, R.: 136-138, 145, 151, 162, 177, 193, 213, 222
Threkeld, M.: 38
Turner, S.: 167, 222
Tzagournis, M.: viii, 62, 64, 138, 169, 171, 175, 177, 178, 198, 203, 222
Union Cemetery: 12
Uniontown: 6-8, 11
United Way: 81, 140, 192, 217
University alumni: 183
University of South Florida: 87, 216
Upham, J.: vii, 52, 60, 209
Upper Arlington: 12, 67, 141, 153, 154, 200
Van Brimmer, B.: vii, 52, 209
Vincent, D.: 1, 20, 24, 66, 131, 180, 222
Vorys, A.: 168
Waltham road residence: 67, 141

Wendy's Restaurants: 136-138, 145, 151, 162, 213, 218
Wheeler, W., of Children's Hospital: 53, 222
Wheeler, W., of the CCC: 91, 222
Wheeling Clinic: 7, 15
White Cross hospital: 56, 143, 156
Wiseman, B.: 53, 54, 132
Wolfe, J., "John Walton": 64, 135, 156, 157, 162, 164, 167, 168, 170
Wooley, C.: vii, 52, 209
Wylie, C.: 151
Yohn, D.: 158, 159, 222
Zollinger, R.: 54-56, 58, 62, 66, 77, 78, 82-87, 129, 131, 132, 182, 213, 217
Zuspan, F.: 116

ABOUT THE AUTHORS

George Paulson, M.D., is Emeritus Professor of Neurology at The Ohio State University. Author of over 250 articles, numerous editorials and chapters, and five books, he is currently a Scholar-in-Residence at the OSU Medical Heritage Center. His major current research interest is in the history of medicine in Central Ohio.

Paulson

Kristin Rodgers, **M.L.I.S.**, Collections Curator of the Medical Heritage Center, The Ohio State University, earned her Bachelor of Arts degree in History of Art from The Ohio State University in 2005 and her Master of Library and Information Science with Archival Studies Specialization from the University of Pittsburgh in 2006. Her research interests are in the health sciences history of Central Ohio and disaster planning.

Rodgers

Authors' photographs courtesy Tom Calovini